Team WORKS!

The Gridiron Playbook for Building a Championship Business Team

"*Teamwork is a vital component for success, and the skill and insight required are vividly portrayed in this book. Give* Team WORKS! *your time and attention, and you will benefit a great deal from your investment.*"
Donald Trump, Chairman & CEO of the Trump Organization (excerpt from Foreword)

"*Having covered Chris since his earliest playing days at Texas A&M, I am not surprised by his business and personal success. Nor am I the least bit surprised that Chris Valletta—one of my all-time favorite quotes—would so eloquently put into words a business book that clearly illustrates the traits that make champions on the football field and in every business field. I absolutely love his sports analogies and how he applies them to business endeavors from Main Street to Wall Street. Chris is a winner, who truly has a game plan for success whether he is wearing a grimy uniform in the trenches on Saturday afternoon or dressed in his power suit for a Monday morning meeting in Manhattan.*"
Rusty Burson, Associate Editor of *12th Man Magazine* at Texas A&M and author of 15 books

"*Chris Valletta's* Team WORKS! *shares the fundamental keys to building a great business with a true focus on the "Little Things..."* *Chris is living proof that practicing the "Little Things" day in and day out builds the foundation for success in everything you do.*"
Warren Barhorst, CEO Iscential

"*After having an opportunity to start multiple businesses and currently in the process of building an internet software company —*

Aajo – I was looking for a way to get a leg-up in the process. Team WORKS! *cleverly associates business with football, giving me new principles I need to manage and motivate the team and ensure that we'll be a champion!"*
Raj Verma, CEO/Founder – Aajo

"Nothing of any consequence happens without the involvement of other people. Wherever you go, you are going to get there with a team. Find out how to make the connections that matter most - and win - with Chris Valletta."
Chris Westfall, National Elevator Pitch Champion and author of *The NEW Elevator Pitch*

"Team WORKS! is an inspiring read on the fundamentals of business principles written from the lens of a competitive professional athlete turned successful businessman and entrepreneur. Chris does a thorough job illustrating how lessons learned while playing professional sports have a direct correlation to business success off the playing field."
Van Adams, Principal at the VanAdams Sports Group

Team
WORKS!

The Gridiron Playbook for
Building a Championship
Business Team

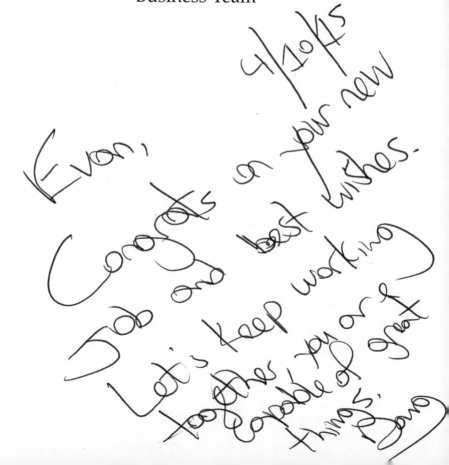

Evan,

Congrats on your new Job and best wishes. Let's keep working together, you are capable of great things.

4/10/15

Dave

Team WORKS!

The Gridiron Playbook for
Building a Championship
Business Team

Chris Valletta

Foreword by
Donald Trump

**BUSINESS
BOOKS**

Winchester, UK
Washington, USA

First published by Business Books, 2014
Business Books is an imprint of John Hunt Publishing Ltd., Laurel House, Station Approach,
Alresford, Hants, SO24 9JH, UK
office1@jhpbooks.net
www.johnhuntpublishing.com

For distributor details and how to order please visit the 'Ordering' section on our website.

Text copyright: Chris Valletta 2013

ISBN: 978 1 78279 669 5

Design: Stuart Davies
www.stuartdaviesart.com

Printed and bound by CPI Group (UK) Ltd, Croydon, CR0 4YY

We operate a distinctive and ethical publishing philosophy in all
areas of our business, from our global network of authors to
production and worldwide distribution.

CONTENTS

Dedication

To my parents, John and Michaela Valletta, who never missed a single game, from Little League to the NFL. Thank you for your love and incredible dedication as parents, for driving me two hours to practices and waiting in the parking lot, for enrolling me in skills camps, for teaching me the value of dedication, discipline and the desire to be as much a champion off the field as on. Your unwavering love and support not only paved the way for me to achieve great things in athletics, but also allowed me the incredible experience of learning what makes a team a TEAM, something that has translated to every facet of my life and without which this book would not be possible.

To my big brother, John Valletta, thank you for being a constant rock of encouragement and support. Thank you for beating me up on the basketball court as kids and teaching me the value of healthy competition. Thank you for seeing me through the toughest times, for standing by me in the best of times and for your incredible strength as a brother, husband, son and father.

To my wife, Lili, thank you for always believing in me, for your never-ending strength, for your constant encouragement, and for loving me for ME. You are the best teammate a guy could ever have. Te amo con todo mi corazon.

To my son, JD. You have changed my life in more ways than you can imagine and have inspired me to a level one could only hope to deserve. May you grow up to become a man of respect, humility and passion – and may you always understand the value of hard work and sacrifice. While my fatherly advice will likely continue for a lifetime, but be memorialized in this text, just remember the cardinal rule of human interaction and teamwork: God gave you two ears and one mouth, which means he wants you to listen twice as much as you speak. I love you, son.

To my incredible friends, business partners and mentors, you have not only been fantastic teammates over the years, but you are truly some of the most incredible Rope-Holders I've ever known. Thank you for your support, coaching and commitment. I am blessed beyond measure to have you in my life.

Foreword

By: Donald Trump

T eam spirit is a necessary ingredient whether you are an entrepreneur or a football coach. Getting things done with the right team can make the difference between a big win and a big loss, whether you're on a television show or working in a corporation. Chris Valletta knows what he's talking about in his book, *Team WORKS!*

I told Chris that I liked his choice for the title, because it has several meanings, and all of them are important. As we've all learned from watching The Apprentice, the teams that work well together always do the best. They have power and momentum, which proves that teamwork *does* work. It also represents collaboration and cooperation, which is a necessary step towards learning the art of negotiation, which is a crucial skill in today's marketplace. Lastly, teamwork also represents what it takes to create and maintain a thriving organization, and as the Chairman and President of The Trump Organization, I know what I'm talking about. Teamwork is a vital component for success, and the skill and insight required are vividly portrayed in this book.

Give *Team WORKS!* your time and attention, and you will benefit a great deal from your investment. And one last word for Chris Valletta: Great job!

Donald Trump
President / CEO
Trump Organization

Team WORKS! – Preface

It was all in my head.

The Infamous Warren Sapp Incident.

It was the fall of 2002 and the New Orleans Saints, my second team in two years, had just released me. I was home in Dallas and going through a bit of an emotional struggle as I decided whether or not to continue my career as an offensive lineman in the National Football League. Most people would say that I was crazy to even be pondering retirement, as playing in the NFL is a rare opportunity and every football player's dream.

NFL life isn't all roses, however, and after the emotional upheaval of two moves and two teams in two years, I started to look toward the future a bit more. When I considered the constant physical struggle associated with maintaining a 305lb offensive lineman's build atop a perpetually sore and battered frame, retirement certainly seemed like an attractive option. On the other hand, I loved football and I loved being a pro football player.

As I licked my wounds and pondered my next step, I was keenly aware of the players' inside joke about what the National Football League's initials really stand for: "Not For Long." There's a great deal of truth buried in the pith – the average player lasts just three years, and there is no such thing as a guaranteed contract. Teams release players all the time, regardless of how much money and time still remains on the contract. All of this churned in my brain as I struggled to arrive at a decision.

One more thing was on my mind: as of the day before, I was officially unemployed. I wasn't treated to a large signing bonus with either of my previous teams, so I wasn't sitting on a pile of cash. My deliberations certainly had a bit of financial urgency to them.

At the height of the emotional turmoil, and after countless phone calls to friends and family for advice, something quite memorable happened. It was 4:30 on a Monday afternoon and I was wandering aimlessly around a department store, eyeballing a Random Celebrity's Deluxe Power Juicer for no apparent reason. Before I could complete my senseless impulse purchase, I received a phone call from my agent. "Congratulations!" he said. "Tampa Bay called a bit ago, and you're now a Buccaneer! I'm booking a flight for you tonight, and you need to report to the practice facility at 5 AM tomorrow morning."

The Deluxe Power Juicer suddenly lost its appeal, and my confusion and consternation dissolved instantly. I was immediately elated – I guess I had wanted to play much more than even I was aware. The celebration officially began, and I left loud messages (something to the effect of "I'M PLAYING BABY!!") on more than a few voicemails.

The icing on the cake was that I was going to be playing for the Tampa Bay Buccaneers in sunny Florida – literally a dream come true for me. Tampa had been in a major transition period, and many analysts felt that the team was extremely well poised for success in the upcoming season. Coach Jon Gruden was in his first year and the team was stacked with talent across every position. Experts predicted that Tampa Bay would make a serious run for the trophy that season. With talent like Keyshawn Johnson, Anthony McFarland, Mike Alstott, Derrick Brooks and, of course, the inimitable Warren Sapp, few argued against the pundits' predictions.

On my way out of the store, I had to pause for a moment to reflect on what had just happened to me. Just a few minutes earlier, I had been wandering around a department store in a daze trying to decide whether I still wanted to continue my career in the NFL. Now, I found myself dashing home to pack my bags for a last-minute flight to join a new NFL franchise. It was a dizzying turn of events, and I was ecstatic. OK, so it wasn't a "guaranteed" multi-million dollar contract with a juicy signing bonus, but it was still a contract to play professional football. And a contract of any sort whatsoever seems pretty appealing when you're currently out of work.

While my mind was instantly transported to Florida, my body was still in Dallas, and my agent called back quickly with the logistical details: my flight left in exactly two hours, and I would have a car waiting for me in Tampa to take me to my hotel, just a mile down the road from the practice facility. He gave me the number of the team staffer who would pick me up at the hotel at 4:30 AM and bring me to the facility to receive my gear. I had a little over thirteen hours to travel half a continent, get some rest, and show up prepared to impress the Tampa coaching staff and my new teammates. The adrenaline hit my veins like a drug.

I had about twenty minutes to dash home, pack, and race to the airport in order to make my flight. I made record time on the highway, and as I moved through security and headed toward my gate, my mind was focused on making a strong first impression with the team. I wanted to let them know by the way I performed during my first practice that I was there to stay. I wanted to make a statement.

I arrived at my gate only to discover that my flight had been delayed. The holdup gave me three hours of dead time, which I filled with agonized finger tapping and knee bouncing. The anticipation was almost unbearable. All I wanted to do was get to Tampa and get on the field, and pressurized thoughts pounded in my head: "I need to make myself known. I need to make a statement. I must show the team that they made a great decision."

After what seemed like a lifetime of waiting at the gate, I finally settled in to a middle seat in the coach section. "Settled" isn't quite the right word, as I was a not-very-svelte 6'3" tall, 305lb NFL lineman with a 22-inch neck. It was most certainly not the most comfortable place to be on the plane, especially for the two other people in my row. But even if I had been seated in first class, there was no way I could have slept during the flight. I was far too excited for my big chance in Tampa. "My time has come," I repeated to myself.

I finally opened the door to my hotel room in Tampa at a little after one in the morning, but at the point when I should have been completely exhausted and ready to crash, something unexpected came over me. Even though I had to meet my driver in a little over three hours, and I should have been climbing in bed for a little sleep, a sudden rush of energy filled my body as I pondered what was happening to me. My dream of playing in the NFL was going to continue, and I felt I had arrived in the very place where my career was finally going to take off. Tampa represented a potential tipping point for me, a place where I could finally be catapulted into NFL stardom. Contemplating the monumental opportunity gave me a gigantic boost of adrenaline. "It's all falling into place," I kept thinking, and I was absolutely overjoyed. I paced around my hotel room, laughing out loud, even jumping up and down.

The next thing I knew, it was 4:15 AM, and I hadn't even peeled back the covers on my hotel room bed. I was operating on zero sleep and pure adrenaline, but somehow, I felt great. "How long can this last?" I wondered.

With a smile on my face and a remarkably springy step given my lack of sleep, I bounded down to the lobby at 4:20 AM to wait for my ride. But the appointed hour came and went, and nobody showed up to take me to the practice facility. As the minutes ticked away, I became more and more anxious. In the NFL, you're NEVER supposed to be late for a meeting, for any reason. Ever. Especially on your first day on the team!

I called my driver several times over the next half hour, but he never answered, and he didn't respond to any of my increasingly frantic messages. I ran up to the front desk and rapidly described my dilemma to the sleepy hotel clerk. He had unwelcome news: the hotel shuttle service hadn't yet started for the day, and the quickest cab company was likely fifteen minutes away. "But," he said, "The Bucs are only a mile up the road. It's probably faster if you walk."

My adrenaline-soaked mind raced: "Surely they know someone was supposed to get me. I'm sure they are still sending someone. Surely they'll understand if I'm a little late. Won't they?" In the end, I decided to make the best of a tenuous situation, and I set off at a dead sprint to get to Buccaneer headquarters as fast as possible.

It was 5:15 AM, and I had been awake all night and operating on pure adrenaline for over twelve hours straight. Twelve hours earlier, I had been an unemployed shopper in the "As Seen On TV" section of a home goods store in Dallas, and was now sprinting in the pre-dawn Florida darkness, late for my first day in my new job as the backup center for the Tampa Bay Buccaneers. The decision to run to the practice facility from the hotel was easy, because I felt like I was running for my life.

Physically exhausted and completely soaked in sweat from the Tampa Bay humidity, I arrived at the facility at 5:23 – exactly eight minutes after I left the hotel (not too bad for a lumbering offensive lineman). I open the main door of the facility and was met immediately by a very put-upon equipment manager who looked like he wanted to kill me.

"Valletta?!" he yelled. It was more an accusation than a question. I answered in the affirmative, and he cut off my attempt at an apology: "I don't give a rat's a** about your excuses! You were supposed to be here at 5am! You're late!" I wasn't off to a great start with my new team.

Sweat from my hands curled the paper of my contract, which I signed while the angry equipment manager worked to fit my helmet. The trainers molded my mouthpiece, and two assistants laced up my shoes and fit my shoulder pads.

As the training staff worked to fit my equipment, other players slowly started to arrive at the field house to get dressed for practice. The veterans all noticed the flurry of activity around me, but my reception wasn't terribly warm. There were more than a few askew glances and sarcastic remarks, and I distinctly remember someone asking, "Whose job did he steal?"

Harsh? Absolutely, but so is life in the NFL. Teams are allotted a fixed number of roster spots, and if a new guy suddenly appears, that means an old guy is no longer on the team. I had no idea who I had replaced – it could have been anyone at any position – but in the eyes of the team, I had taken a precious roster slot from one of their own.

I felt self-conscious and very alone. Most of the time, players in my situation have the luxury of knowing at least a couple of people on the team from college or previous NFL teams, but I didn't know a soul. I felt every bit the outsider. This only added fuel to the adrenaline-fueled fire that was already burning inside me, and I felt an even stronger desire to make a statement. I was nervous and uncomfortable, but I told myself, "After today, they will all know who I am."

I wasn't wrong.

Before I knew it, I was lined up in formation with my new teammates to begin the stretching exercises that marked the beginning of my first practice with the Tampa Bay Buccaneers. Head Coach Jon Gruden welcomed me to his team with a slap on the helmet. "Let's go to work son," he said. Suddenly, my lack of sleep didn't matter, the predawn sprint to the practice facility didn't matter, and the strange looks and snide comments from the veterans didn't matter – the only thing that mattered to me was making the best impression possible when it came time to perform.

As the stretching session came to a close, Coach Gruden announced the first practice event: "Post-stretch, seven on seven, second string offense against first string defense. Let's go!" Sometimes referred to as the "inside drill," seven on seven is a drill in which the offensive linemen, tight ends, quarterback and running backs square off against the defensive linemen, defensive ends, and linebackers. This is a brutally tough drill that separates the men from the boys – helmet to helmet, facemask to facemask. On the NFL practice field, seven on seven is the ultimate test of mettle. "It's my time," I repeated to myself.

It did seem a little strange that Coach Gruden would choose to start practice with this extremely intense full-contact exercise. Normally, teams start with lower intensity drills, and slowly work their way up in intensity as the practice progresses, but apparently Coach Gruden's plan was for us to jump right in and start pounding each other. No matter – I intended to rise to the occasion and prove myself worthy of the contract I had signed minutes before.

As the backup (second string) center, I was thrust into the huddle with the remainder of the second string offense. As I shook hands and introduced myself to my new teammates, I had a keen awareness that I was in the most intense situation I had ever faced on the gridiron. I was about to square off in my first seven on seven drill against the starting defense for the Tampa Bay Buccaneers, with my future hanging in the balance. It would have been easy to shrink from the magnitude of the moment, but instead it just caused another bucket of adrenaline to hit my bloodstream. I was keyed up like never before in my life, and the seven on seven drill was the perfect opportunity to channel all of my energy and drive into making sure the coaches knew who I was. This was going to be my big moment!

I received the play in the huddle: a simple counter play to the weak (left) side. My job was to block the defensive nose guard – in this case, a gentleman named Warren Sapp. One of the best defensive linemen in professional football history, Warren was known for his gaudy compilation of quarterback sacks and his absolute fierceness on the field. He ultimately finished his career with the second-highest sack count in the NFL record books, and today, Warren is enshrined in the NFL's Hall of Fame. Needless to say, even at the time, Warren's reputation certainly preceded him.

"OK," I said to myself, "if I'm going to make a big first impression, why not make it against one of the best defensive linemen in the history of the NFL?" We broke the huddle and I sprinted to the line of scrimmage. The others moved at a slow walk, and my comical eagerness elicited a few snide remarks about my likeness to "Rudy," the walk-on defensive end for Notre Dame who, despite being too slow, too short, and too weak, managed to out-hustle everyone to earn a spot on the team. I was too keyed up to pay much attention, however, as I stood eye to eye with a living legend of defensive football.

Warren welcomed me to the team as only he could: "Who the he** is this guy and what the f*** is he doing on my field? Who are you?" My heart pounded in my chest, and I stared at him with hate in my eyes. Warren didn't let up in the slightest. "Do you speak? What are you looking at? Are you an idiot?"

The jawing continued, and it was beyond colorful. Warren's considerable playing ability was eclipsed only by his exceptionally well-developed tongue, which was known to unleash verbal onslaughts capable of peeling paint. Warren's game was not only about out-playing, out-hustling and out-working his opponents, but also about getting inside their heads. Sapp viewed intimidation as an art form, and he was absolutely merciless, but I wasn't about to give any ground to him. My future was on the line. The longer his tongue-lashing continued, the more determined I became to turn his trash talking into respect.

I was a smoldering volcano about to erupt. I grew angrier, more motivated, and more fired up, and the emotions amplified when I thought of the enormous opportunity in front of me: if I could crush the best defensive tackle in football on my first play as a Buccaneer, I would solidify my position on this team and etch my name into the coaches' minds as a player worthy of keeping around for a long time.

I bent over in my stance and grabbed the football. As I gripped the ball in preparation to snap it to backup quarterback Brad Johnson, I began to go numb with adrenaline. My hands started to shake with anticipation as I mentally prepared myself for the most important play in my career.

This was it – it all came down to this moment. Brad called the signals that would start the play: "Black 28! Blaaaaaack 28! Set, HUT!!!"

With piston-like force, I snapped the ball and fired off the line of scrimmage like a rocket, with the top of my helmet aimed at the center of Warren Sapp's chest. I made contact with the 6'5", 340-lb defensive tackle in what felt like the most perfect hit of my life. It felt absolutely clean, like a driver hitting a golf ball square and true, and over the sound of our pads cracking together, I heard the breath driven out of Warren's chest by the force of the blow. I continued to drive my legs with all of my strength, and I felt Sapp's feet leave the ground. Driving my feet harder and harder, I pushed with the full force of the hopes and dreams of a long and lucrative NFL career in front of me. Sapp continued his fall, and I drove him into the ground with all of my weight.

I couldn't believe it - I had just "pancaked" Warren Sapp! A "pancake" block is when the defender winds up flat on his back, staring up at the sky in a daze. They don't happen very often, but when they do, pancake blocks are spectacular. Conversely, "getting pancaked" is the worst possible situation for a defensive lineman, because he knows it will be replayed forever in the highlight reels. I had just subjected Tampa's all-star defensive tackle to the humiliation of getting flattened. I was beside myself with elation. I had crushed one of the best defensive linemen in NFL history on my very first play as a Buccaneer!

After I slammed Sapp into the ground and landed on top of him, I thrust myself up off his defeated body, pointed my finger in his face, and yelled "WHOOOOOOOAAAAAAAA!" I have absolutely no idea where this came from, but I had just unleashed enough pent-up energy to power a small city, and for some reason I felt the best way to round out the experience would be to rub it in the future Hall-of-Famer's face in front of the entire team.

As I sprung to my feet in self-proclaimed victory, I noticed every player on the team standing dumbfounded around me, watching me the way a chicken might watch a card trick: they were more than a little confused. The thrill of my victory vanished and all the air left my lungs as I slowly realized what I had just done.

To my enduring embarrassment, I finally grasped that Coach Gruden hadn't actually called for a full-contact seven on seven drill after the team finished stretching. Instead, he had called for the seven on seven *walk-through* drill. In a walk-through drill, players just review their responsibilities and move to their positions at a somewhat leisurely pace.

There's no hitting in a walk-through.

No wonder I had pancaked Warren – he wasn't expecting my ferocious hit because there wasn't supposed to be any hitting whatsoever in this particular drill! The poor guy had literally stood there while I fired off the line of scrimmage and tried to rip his head off. Not only that, but after I caught him completely off guard and flattened him in front of the entire team, I screamed in his face and taunted him like an idiot.

Needless to say, Sapp was not impressed with his new teammate. He did not have a placid disposition in the first place, but he went absolutely crazy. He leapt to his feet, ripped my helmet off of my head, and began trying to bash my now-exposed noggin with it. My deep embarrassment quickly turned to real fear, as a football helmet is a heavy, hard object, and a man Sapp's size could easily crush my skull with one blow if any of his wild swings connected. I did what any sane person would have done in the same circumstances: I ran away from the enraged giant.

I had certainly made a statement.

While the situation eventually calmed down, and we were finally able to resume the practice session, I hadn't quite made the first impression I'd hoped. Thankfully, Coach Gruden didn't run me off, but I emerged from my first day as a Buccaneer with a $100 fine and a badly bruised ego.

What went wrong? How did I manage to turn an enormous opportunity into a near-catastrophe, despite my best intentions and all the motivation in the world? I had unwittingly violated a couple of sacred rules of athletics and business, which we'll cover in detail in the coming pages. Together with other critically important concepts, these rules form the backbone of my time-tested process for building what I call "championship business teams," organizations that dominate their markets and leave their competition in the dust. By the time you're done reading this book, I think you'll have both the understanding and the confidence to begin assembling your own championship business team and start accelerating your climb to the top of your market.

My athletic career spanned over twenty years, and I have always been amazed at the way the tenets of athletic success translate seamlessly to every other aspect of life. The discipline of my athletic life carries over to this day in everything I do, and it has become obvious to me as I have enjoyed a series of successes in the business world that the lessons, skills, attributes, and work habits that brought me athletic success are also the reason for my business attainments. From my health to my personal relation-ships, there is not one aspect of my life that hasn't been profoundly shaped by the lessons I learned on the athletic field.

This book is your inside ticket to the locker rooms, war rooms and strategy sessions of the best players and the best teams in business and athletics. Consider it to be your all-access pass to understanding what goes into making a championship team in both the athletic and business worlds. I'd like for you to view it as a playbook for developing your own championship team. I'll outline the principles that have worked wonders for me on the gridiron and in the boardroom.

In the first segment, I'll cover the all-important starting point to becoming the leader of your own world-class team: *you*. I'll distill the hard-taught lessons of twenty years of athletic success and fifteen years of business achievement into the unvarnished essentials. Master the concepts and master yourself, and you'll be on your way to mastering your market.

In the second section, I'll describe my time-tested approach to recruiting, hiring, training, and preparing my championship teams for game day. I'll tell you about the crucial difference between finding great players and finding the *right* players, and I'll tell you how I ensure that my talented team members truly become a team. The greatest successes are accessible only to cohesive teams, and I'll give you what I've found to be a priceless roadmap to creating a team with a championship mindset and skill set.

In the last section, we'll discuss how to approach the Big Game. Your "game day" may be a critical client meeting, sales pitch, board meeting, product rollout, marketing plan, or other high-stakes business activity – just like my big games are nowadays – and I'll cover the game day leadership lessons I've adapted from some of the greatest coaches and players in college and professional sports.

Finally, I'll tie it all together with what I believe to be the *sine qua non* of business and athletic success. Every other championship attribute that we'll discuss is absolutely necessary for success, but together they are all still insufficient without this *one key ingredient* that only world-class teams possess.

In the coming pages, I'm going to let you in on the lessons that have brought me a lifetime of athletic and business success. Following these tenets brings terrific success to my ongoing business efforts, and by the time you turn the last page in this book, you'll have the tools, mindset, and framework you need in order to build your own championship business team.

Let's get started!

PART 1

THE MINDSET

Team WORKS! – Chapter 1

Player, Coach, Manager, or all of the above?

You'll wear a few hats simultaneously. Wear them well!

I love football, and I love business. I have a passion for the effort, sweat, struggle, and amazing highs that both football and business bring. Both pursuits demand your heart, mind, and soul, and there is no room for half-measures or conditional commitment. Business and football both require you to slide all your chips to the center of the table and work your tail off to make the absolute best of the hand you're dealt. I love the risks and rewards, and I enjoy the highs and lows of the journey.

Making your way on the gridiron and in the boardroom requires deep dedication, relentless persistence, and intense love for what you're doing. I felt profoundly alive when I stepped out onto the football field before kickoff and smelled the freshly cut grass, heard the roar of 80,000 voices, strapped on my helmet, and prepared to do battle. There's usually less adrenaline in the business environment, but I feel a very similar sense of purpose and aliveness as I strive to continue creating championship business teams.

Since you picked up this book, I suspect that your perspective is at least a little bit similar to mine. You probably have athletic experience somewhere in your background, and you can probably appreciate the sense of visceral connection and immediacy that athletics brings. I am an entrepreneur largely because I crave the realness, risk, effort, teamwork, and reward that building and running a successful company shares in common with sports. Maybe you feel the same way – if a major college or pro football game is a microcosm of the business world, containing spectators, support staff, analysts, and regulators in addition to the players on the field, you probably can't imagine being anything other than one of the gladiators.

If I've described you accurately, then you're in the right spot. In the coming pages, we'll further explore the many parallels between football and business. Even if football isn't your sport of choice, I think you'll find that the concepts translate almost universally, so I'd like you to treat this book like your playbook –

the all-important document that contains a team's strategy and tactics – for building a championship business team.

We'll discuss what I believe to be the best way to recruit, train, prepare, motivate, and lead a championship business team. I've been on over a hundred different athletic and business teams in my life, and many of the teams I've led have achieved terrific successes. I'm passionate about the power of teamwork and I'm convinced that the biggest successes in life are only accessible to well-constructed, well-led, and well-prepared teams.

It may not seem like teamwork is a big deal, but I believe it is the hidden ingredient in every successful business in every market on the planet. Whether it's your favorite burger chain, gourmet restaurant, or coffee shop, or your favorite online retailer, service provider, or auto repair shop, you can bet your paycheck that there's a high-performance team firing on all eight cylinders behind the scenes.

Speaking of firing on all eight cylinders, there is no individual more synonymous with success than NASCAR's Richard Petty. Although auto racing may seem to be an individual sport – after all, there is only one person inside the race car banging doors with competitors and making split-second decisions in high intensity racing situations – winning on race day is every bit a team affair. Here's what the most successful driver in NASCAR history has to say about teamwork:

In his own words: Mr. Richard Petty, 7-time NASCAR and Daytona 500 Champion.

In racing, as in life and most anything you do, it takes an entire team to be successful. 'Richard Petty' is just one person and I wouldn't be here if it weren't for the people around me. It took everything and everyone working together, towards the same goal, in our case to win races, for everything to come together and be successful. That's teamwork, everyone pulling in one direction and making the best out of it.

I just drove the car, but we had my brother (Maurice) build the engine, my cousin (Dale Inman) work on the car, and everyone else in the shop to make it all go. And we all had the same purpose, and that was to win races. Everyone knew their role and we showed up to the track each week and did it. We'd then go onto the next race and do the same thing. We may disagree here and there, but for the most part you just trusted what everyone had to do. There was no way that I could do it all myself. We all had to do our own little thing and do it the best we could. We just had all the pieces fit and everyone moved in the right direction. We really trusted each other too. And today each of us is in the NASCAR Hall of Fame because of our success in each of our own little area.

With 200 victories, Richard Petty is the winningest driver in NASCAR in history. He won the Daytona 500 seven times, and he is a 7-time NASCAR series champion. Richard is an inaugural inductee of the NASCAR Hall of Fame, and is the recipient of the Presidential Medal of Freedom.

Teamwork isn't indispensable only in the high-stakes games of NASCAR racing and professional sports. Teamwork is just as critical to success in businesses we interact with on a daily basis. In my dad's business, hotel management, top-notch teamwork is the driving force behind a successful operation:

In his own words: Mr. John Valletta, President, Super 8 Worldwide, Inc. and President, Howard Johnson International, Inc.

"What is that bright light shining on me?"

To the average traveling consumer, the concept of managing a small hotel or motel probably seems relatively simple. After all, what is there to do? You clean the room, you rent the room, you take the money to the bank. Then you repeat the cycle all over again the next day and the next day and the next. Lather, rinse, repeat... just like the shampoo bottle says.

But there really is much more to it, particularly if that hotel is small, and perhaps family owned and operated with just a few other employees.

For starters, how many businesses come to mind that sell a product with a shelf life of only 24 hours? You may be hard pressed to think of one. In the food business, ice cream will melt in minutes after it is sold but will keep for weeks in inventory if it's kept frozen. Canned food products can last for years, dairy products for weeks, and even fresh produce will last for several days before it spoils. New cars can sit on the lot for months before they are finally sold, and electronics will typically become obsolete, but certainly not unsaleable, if they don't sell right away. For almost all consumer products, if you don't sell it today you'll try to sell it tomorrow.

But not a hotel room. Think about it. Every day, any room that isn't sold by midnight is gone – forever. You can't sell yesterday's room today or tomorrow. Every night at midnight, today's unsold inventory simply goes away. Lost opportunity forever. So the hotel operator, every day, has only one short 24 hour period to sell 100% of his or her product. And a lot of things can get in the way. To accomplish the goal of being 'sold out' takes enormous teamwork among all the departments in the hotel: the reception desk, the telephone operator, the maintenance department, the laundry staff, housekeeping, the courtesy van driver, the breakfast attendant. All of this goes on 24 hours a day, 7 days a week, 52 weeks a year. After all, who has ever seen a hotel that closes at night, or perhaps on holidays, like a department store or a hair salon?

Now consider that, in many small hotels, all those departments might be staffed by a grand total of only 5 or 6 individuals, all responsible for several tasks, all needing to be properly trained to do multiple jobs and all dependent on each other to ensure that, every day, every room is ready for new guests and is in what we like to refer to as NEPG (No Evidence of Prior Guests) condition. It is a daunting task, one that simply cannot be accomplished by any individual alone. The general manager, and the hotel, can succeed only with the support of a strong team. Kind of like the turtle that finds itself on top of a fencepost. It's not sure how it got there, but it knows it had to have had a lot of help.

After over 40 years of carrying bags, checking guests in and out, managing, owning and operating hotels and running hotel brands, I've learned that the "recipe for success" isn't necessarily complicated but it is hard work that requires discipline, entrepreneurial determination, collaboration, coordination, occasionally a bit of good fortune (although it's my experience that most "good luck" is self-created and not found) and most critical – teamwork. No different than the recipe for success for a football team playing for a Super Bowl championship or a sailing team racing for the America's cup.

In the hotel, if a room isn't clean guests will complain and not return. So the executive housekeeper must ensure that every room has been put together perfectly. If a housekeeping team member doesn't show up for work – something that can happen often - room availability will be delayed. So flexible scheduling and staff members able to come to work on a moment's notice, if needed, is a requirement. If the laundry equipment breaks down on the maintenance engineer's day off there must be a backup plan. If the phone isn't answered promptly because one of the front desk receptionists called in sick, the caller will hang up and call the hotel next door. That's lost opportunity and a lost sale, intolerable with a consumer product that "goes bad" in 24 hours. The interdepartmental and interpersonal dependencies in the hotel are many, as is the need for multi-tasking cross-trained employees ready to "jump in and do whatever it takes".

And you thought it was just 'clean the room, rent the room, go to the bank'!

When I was a 16 year old bellman one of my managers once told me that, regardless of what was going on "behind the scenes", the hotel business was like show business. To our guests, all the employees were always "onstage" and had to project an image of confidence and happiness, regardless of how screwed up things were in the back office or down in the room service kitchen. It's not quite that easy anymore. Today's hotel manager works in a fully transparent environment in which anyone can say anything, right or wrong, good or bad, about their experience at a hotel by means of social media and the dozens of ratings and review websites now online. We can't hide, nor should we be able to hide, our flaws and our weaknesses. Serve a bad meal in the restaurant and the world will know about it – in minutes! Wi-Fi speed is slow? Plan on reading bad reviews about it. Or maybe last night's guest smoked in a non-smoking room? Definitely not a NEPG situation and definitely one that will earn a bad review. Long before a potential guest has made a reservation he or she has read several online reviews about the hotel -probably at least 5 or 6 -and maybe several more if he or she comes across one that's not so good. And so the general manager is faced with yet one more challenge in the quest to sell all of today's inventory before it "expires" at midnight.

Little that happens in a hotel happens "as planned", and the staff must be able to adapt accordingly. Regardless of the situation, our job is always to exceed the expectations of every guest. If an unexpected busload of senior citizens pulls up to the front door of the hotel's restaurant at noon for lunch, it's too late to schedule a meeting to discuss how to handle such an event. If the airport shuttle van breaks down on the way to pick up a group of corporate executives, someone needs to be resourceful enough to get them into taxis immediately – and pay for it – without having to call the GM for approval. Successful managers recognize that in today's transparent environment they need the support of a dedicated and flexible core team of employees who are empowered to solve problems on the spot. Take care of the little things and the big things will take care of themselves.

I checked into a hotel one evening a couple of years ago and asked the front desk receptionist for an extra bag of coffee for the coffeemaker in my room. She was extremely polite, efficient and courteous and, when she finally couldn't find one anywhere, she was very apologetic. Not a big deal to me and I told her so. There was one in the room and it would be adequate. Imagine my surprise when, about 5 minutes after I settled into my room, there was a knock on my door. It was that same young lady, with two bags of coffee in her hand. "Here you go Mr. Valletta. My manager is watching the desk for me. We didn't want you to be disappointed". I was astounded. After all, she had already handled it well. It would have been easy to just forget about it. What a terrific team member she was. I could tell the effort was genuine, and it was the difference between a happy customer and a very impressed happy customer. You can't train that kind of attitude into anyone. It's got to be there when you hire the person. And it's got to start at the top with whoever is leading the team. I've told that story a thousand times and every time I tell it, it makes me smile.

Teamwork is the heart and soul of the hotel business. For any general manager to be successful and generate results there must be a cohesive team ready to support him or her. Or, to use the words of someone that was on my team a few years ago, "John, our job is to make your job easier. Remember, we all shine by reflected light".

John Valletta has worked exclusively in the hotel industry since the age of 16, beginning as a bellman and working up through many roles until being promoted to his first general manager position at the age of 21. He has been employed since 2002 by Wyndham Hotel Group, the world's largest hotel company, where he serves as president of the Super 8® and Howard Johnson® brands.

There is no long-term success in business without highly effective teamwork, but we have one extremely important topic to cover before we can dive into the specifics of how to create a winning business team: YOU!

You might not have seen that coming. After all, this is a book about teamwork, and you found this book in the business section, not the personal development section! All of that notwithstanding, if you are serious about developing a championship business team, it's important to realize that *you* are the most important component of your team.

Why? Because it's *your* team. You will evaluate the prospects and select the players. You will design the training programs, internships, and professional development opportunities that will prepare your players for success. You will lead the preparation efforts for upcoming business events, and you will establish the daily business dynamics that will form the backdrop and set the tone for your team's success. You will strategically position your business in your market, and your team will look to you to lead by example.

As you probably noticed, there's bound to be a lot of "you" in your team. It's your baby.

No pressure.

Don't worry though. While you will never develop a championship business team without developing impeccable personal habits for success, I think that there are only two things you need to do in order to attain personal excellence in your chosen enterprise: pay close attention to the Little Things, and commit to the daily practice of mastering yourself. That's it. Nothing more.

And absolutely nothing less.

Because those are steps one and two on the road to building a championship business team, they're the first two things we'll discuss in Chapters two and three. As we do, I'd like you to keep in mind that when you commit to learning how to master the details of your industry, and you make the decision to learn how to master your mindset and emotions, you're committing to a process that never stops. If you're truly dedicated to personal excellence, you'll never wake up and say, "I've finally graduated from Me University, and there are no more rungs available for me to climb on my own personal ladder to greatness." If you're ever even remotely tempted to say something like that, take my word for it: you're doing it wrong.

Before we begin exploring those two topics in earnest, we have an important question to answer: who are you? I'm not raising an existential question about your sense of self; I'm really asking about what role you'll be playing as you begin developing and leading your championship team. While football offers us many nearly-perfect parallels with the business world, the modern football milieu unfortunately falls a little bit short of providing us with a single role or position that accurately reflects the kinds of tasks you'll be handling.

As I've already mentioned, a huge part of your responsibility is to set the strategic direction for your team, establish and enforce the standards and best practices that will characterize your business, train your team, make tactical "game day" decisions about how to best pursue business opportunities, and use your expertise and insight to make the necessary adjustments in your game plan after kickoff in order to give you the best chance of winning. Your to-do list sounds very much like the job description of a head coach in today's football world.

But that's not all you'll be doing. You'll also be recruiting, evaluating, hiring, and sometimes firing the personnel who will eventually comprise your championship team. You'll evaluate their performance, change their positions on your team, and adjust their responsibility levels as you watch them grow and learn over time. You'll also select, train, and evaluate your "assistant coaches," the various department heads and team leads that every business needs in order to survive and thrive.

That sounds a lot like the general manager in today's NFL.

It doesn't stop there, either. In addition to the strategic, administrative, and supervisory roles you'll play within the organizational structure of your business, you'll also be doing something no modern coach or manager ever does: you'll actually be on the field! *You* will represent your entire company in important negotiations, *you* will pitch your products and services to shareholders and potential clients, *you* will ensure that your business follows all required regulations, and *you* will be on the ground ensuring that your operations and support functions deliver on the promises you made during your marketing and sales efforts.

Clearly, you won't be just any player. You'll also be much more than a team captain, who acts as the coach's representative on the field. You'll actually *be* the coach – and general manager – while you're battling away in the trenches! While this kind of role doesn't have a clear equivalent in the modern football world, there is a terrific parallel role from the game's bygone era: the player-coach.

Have you ever heard of Lambeau Field? It's possibly the most famous professional football venue in use today, home of the Green Bay Packers. It was named after Curly Lambeau, who was Green Bay's player-coach for many years. He led his teams to a record six championships, a feat matched only by Chicago's George Halas, the winningest player-coach in history. No matter which side of the Chicago vs. Green Bay fence you prefer (it's one of the most longstanding and hard-fought rivalries in all of professional sports, and fans on both sides are absolutely fanatical), you can look to both Curly Lambeau and "Papa Bear" Halas as your player-coach paragons. They called the shots from down in the trenches, just like you'll do. And while your city may not name a stadium in your honor when it's all said and done, I'm confident you'll achieve massive business success if you remain committed to the principles I'll outline in the coming pages.

So, player-coach, it's time to get to work!

Team WORKS! – Chapter 2

The Little Things

A Championship Business Team has a laser focus on the fundamental details.

I was fifteen years old, 6'2" tall, and weighed 260 pounds when I strapped on a football helmet for the first time as a high school football player in Windham, New Hampshire.

I had no idea what I was doing.

Comical as it sounds, I actually put my shoulder pads on backwards, and I installed my knee pads upside down. I left my mouthpiece – an important piece of gear designed to prevent my teeth from shattering after a collision with another player – sitting in the bottom of my locker. I was lost. I didn't have the first clue about what to do, where to go, or what to think.

To avoid further embarrassment, I focused on paying very close attention to the other players in the locker room, and tried to follow exactly what they were doing in order to get properly dressed for practice. At a bare minimum, I wanted to ensure I was properly protected. Even more than that, I wanted to ensure I wasn't a laughingstock on my first day as a football player.

I wasn't just big for my age; I was a gigantic high school freshman. On the surface, my size would appear to give me a distinct advantage in a game that consists mostly of using size, strength and leverage to impose one's will on other players. For the most part, this is true. However, in the game of football, incorrect technique is a serious health risk, and big guys are just as vulnerable as smaller guys. Simply put, if you don't know what you're doing, you can get hurt seriously.

Unlike 90% of the other players on the practice field that day, I had never played the game before. New Hampshire offered numerous little-league football opportunities (Pee-Wee, Pop Warner, and grade school leagues abounded), with one important restriction: kids over a certain weight weren't allowed to play, because of the greater injury risk it would pose to the smaller kids. I spent the entirety of my childhood well beyond the maximum weight limit for little league football. As a result, soccer, baseball, track, and basketball were my sports of choice growing up, and high school was the first opportunity I had to play football.

Because of my inexperience, I was at a distinct disadvantage, and I looked enviously at the more experienced kids who knew what they were doing. Despite my intimidating size, I felt fear, intimidation, and nerves creeping their way into my body.

"You gain strength, courage, and confidence by every experience in which you really stop to look fear in the face. You must do the thing which you think you cannot do."
~ Eleanor Roosevelt

I gathered myself, took a deep breath, and stepped onto the football field for the first time. It didn't take long for the coaches to recognize my athletic ability; unfortunately, they also noticed my complete lack of football technique. I was a bit scared and way too timid, but even at this early stage in my football career, I was convinced that I could become a great player if someone would take the time to teach me.

Before long, my head coach pulled me to the sideline to teach me the absolute basics, the little details that underpinned all athletic movement on the football field. He focused on two areas: the stance, or body position football players hold just prior to the start of a play and from which all technique begins, and hitting – the act of crashing your body into your opponent's body with the intent of knocking him over.

Step 1: The Stance

Every play in a football game starts with each player lining up alongside his teammates and facing the opponent, then assuming the physical posture required both by the rules of the game and by the rules of physics. A player's stance on the football field is like a dancer's "hold" position (many people are surprised to learn that a number of the best football players take ballet classes to enhance their balance, coordination, and flexibility). Each position has a particular stance that's designed for maximum effect. Wide receivers take a stance that helps them sneak past their defender and sprint downfield. Running backs take a stance that allows them to move quickly to either side at the start of the play. As a lineman, I needed to learn how to take a stance that allowed me to move quickly in *any* direction at the start of the play.

Because the stance influences how quickly a player can move from the starting position to perform his assigned role during the play, it's a critically important element to master in order to enjoy any appreciable football success. Just as importantly, an undisciplined stance can inadvertently "tip off" the defense about the direction of the play. Astute defenders may notice how your body is positioned, or which direction you're leaning, or where your eyes are focused, which may take away the element of surprise and jeopardize the success of the play.

My coach took me aside for a brief but thorough crash course in the ABCs of proper alignment, stance, and steps, and then moved quickly on to Step 2: hitting.

Step 2: Hitting

Football is a game of crashing into one another at high-velocities with bad intentions. Many think that football is nothing more than a field of 22 men locked in a barbaric battle, and they're not entirely wrong - football is certainly a violent game. But it's also a highly calculated, meticulously coordinated game of strategy and execution. Imagine a chess game comprised of eleven pieces per side, only in this particular game, the pieces are allowed to knock each other over. Before I could begin to learn the chess-like strategy of football, I had to learn how to win the individual battles against my defensive counterparts, which is what my coach focused on during this phase of our training session.

The "hit" is a basic element of the game, used to either bring the opposing team's ball carrier to the ground (called a "tackle"), or to prevent – or "block" - the other team's players from tackling your team's ball carrier. Hitting correctly requires a very specific technique that allows you to deliver the greatest impact to your target, but in a way that doesn't jeopardize the safety of your head, neck and back. My coach spent a significant amount of time teaching me the technique for properly delivering and receiving hits. After 20 solid minutes of practice against a football sled (a large, sturdy pad in the shape of an opposing player, attached to skis, which allows football players to practice their hitting technique), he declared me ready to take the field.

Before sending me on my way, however, my coach assured me that he would help me gradually develop the knowledge of what to do, where to go, and how to react, and that the only thing I had to worry about at the moment was becoming familiar with basic football technique. It was comforting to have the daunting task of learning how to play football broken down into very simple steps, and I felt much less anxious after my coach taught me that I only had one focus during my first days as a football player: to master the basics of body position and hitting technique.

My comfort was short-lived, disappearing the nanosecond I received my first hit, which felt like a car wreck. In the brief flash of pain and disbelief that accompanied my first football collision, I wondered what in the world I had signed up for, and I seriously doubted whether I would last the entire practice session, much less the entire season. It seemed absurdly painful, and I didn't think there was any way I could do it even once more, much less thousands more times.

But to my surprise, I quickly recovered from my initial shock, and I discovered something strange: I really liked hitting! I naturally took to the rough-and-tumble nature of the game, and I quickly fell in love with the sport. It was equal parts finesse and brute force, and I found that the more I focused on the fundamentals of footwork and hitting technique, the more rapidly I attained success. These two details were used every single day, on every single play, and mastering them was the key to mastering the game.

"Never be afraid to try something new. Remember, amateurs built the ark, professionals built the Titanic."
~ Unknown

I had a solid sense of how important it was to become great at the fundamentals in order to be a successful football player, but it wasn't until I met an offensive line coach by the name of J.B. Grimes that I came to fully understand this truth: **perfect fundamentals make champions.** Coach Grimes' influence not only shaped my football technique, but would also come to shape the way I approach every aspect of my business life as well.

I first met J.B. Grimes at the end of my sophomore year at Texas A&M University. Coach Grimes is one of the most famous and respected position coaches in the country, and he had just arrived to be our offensive line coach. He is tough, fair, and passionate about the game, and he has a flair for both teaching his players and igniting their passion.

When I first saw him, I was less than impressed. Most offensive line coaches look much like their charges: they're usually very large humans. It's much easier to gain the attention and respect of men that are 6'3 or taller, and 300 pounds or heavier, when you can go toe-to-toe with them physically. At about 5-foot 9 and 175 pounds, Coach Grimes struck me as possibly the least likely person on earth to be an offensive line coach. But what Coach Grimes lacked in stature, he more than made up in his knowledge and his love for the game. He was relentless, and he lived, breathed, ate, and slept football.

In our first meeting with Coach Grimes, we couldn't help but notice an enormous sign that he had installed on the wall. It read:

"THE LITTLE THINGS"

This gigantic sign hung front and center in the room, and measured about 5 feet long by 3 feet tall. It was impossible to even walk by the offensive linemen's meeting room without being reminded of Coach Grimes' fanatical obsession with the small things, the fundamentals of the game. To this day, Coach Grimes firmly believes that the success of the team depends on each and every player mastering the little details of the game. His philosophy is simple: if you do the smallest things perfectly, day in and day out, without hesitation, you'll beat your opponent 99% of the time.

To Coach Grimes, The Little Things mean the difference between winning and losing. He started every practice by working on the basic fundamentals of the game. He took his offensive line through a series of basic drills not unlike the one my high school coach took me through during my very first football practice. Under his watchful eye, some of the finest offensive linemen in college football rehearsed the absolute basics – the Little Things – before every practice. We were some of the most talented offensive linemen in the country, with years of experience and numerous all-state and all-American accolades to our credit, yet Coach Grimes made us practice elements that were almost embarrassingly basic – and he made us do it every day! He cut us absolutely no slack, demanding perfection in our stance, hand position, foot position, weight distribution, step alignment, and much more.

Needless to say, J.B. burned the fundamentals into our collective consciousness, and over time, doing the Little Things right came to feel as natural as breathing. His efforts paid off in spades. What we considered to be Pee-Wee league drills ended up being nothing of the sort – those exercises became the essential ingredient to building one of the best offensive lines in college football.

The Little Things automatically became part of every single play. The repetition caused an instinctive habit to form – so much so that, to this day, I still sometimes have dreams about doing the Little Things with Coach Grimes watching closely!

In his own words: Coach J.B. Grimes

When I started coaching high school football in 1977, I was armed with two things: passion and aggressiveness. I didn't know "come here" from "sic 'em" about fundamentals, techniques, and details. My approach was just to tell my players to "fire off the ball and block that dude in front of you," and that's about all I had to offer at the time.

My cave-man approach went on for about four years – two as a high school coach and two as a graduate assistant under Texas A&M great John David Crow. I guess Coach Crow took a liking to me because he did something for me that changed me as an offensive line coach, and changed the path of my career. He somehow got me a job at the University of Arkansas under head coach Lou Holtz.

Coach Holtz and his offensive line coach, Larry Beightol, introduced me to "The Little Things" and the philosophy that lies behind the words: **if you take care of the little things, the big things will take care of themselves!**

Those are great words to live by, and I believe in them with all the passion and aggressiveness that I still have in me. But over the years the Little Things have taken on an even deeper meaning for me – not just as a football coach, but also as a husband and father. I don't care if it's your marriage, your business, or your football team, it's the foundation that counts.

I've heard it said that we stumble over pebbles, not mountains, and it stands to reason that if it's the small things that trip you up, it's also the small things that build you up. You don't start building a home by putting the roof on first. You start with the foundation, and that's what the Little Things are all about.

There's a lot of grey in life and in football – especially after the ball is snapped. As a coach, my job is to make it as black and white as possible – to take the grey out – before the ball is snapped, so that my players know exactly what to do when the play starts. Taking the grey out before the ball is snapped gives you a much more effective and efficient player post-snap, after all hell breaks loose!

To do this, there are a couple of things that absolutely must take place. Number one, we've all got to be talking the same language and working for the same goals. Number two, the fundamentals have to be drilled into us until they become automatic. After the snap, instinct takes over, and the instinct has to be right every time.

*Most offensive line coaches spend time teaching their players who to block and why to block that particular player. Then, if time permits, they tell their players **how** to block. I think that's completely backwards! I believe players must know how to do the basics – the Little Things – as perfectly as possible. The essence of coaching lies in the "how". When that's done, the "who" and "why" are easy.*

Time and time again I have had former players call or write to tell me the impact of the Little Things on their lives and careers. As I get further into my career (starting my 37th season!) I quite frankly hammer them home more now than ever. In my profession (and I suspect this is true of most professions), there are schemers and there are fundamentalists. I am the latter. Even though there are "gurus" out there I believe it will always come down to fundamentals.

I jokingly tell people that the last truly great breakthrough in football was when Knute Rockne threw that forward pass. I imagine the other team's reaction was "What the hell was that?!" But ever since then, it has always been about the fundamentals of blocking and tackling, and I believe it will always come down to the fundamentals in business, relationships, and in life.

JB Grimes is the Offensive Line Coach at Auburn

University. In his 35 years as an NCAA coach, JB's teams have participated in 15 bowl games and won 6 conference championships. He helped coach the 1987 Louisiana-Monroe team to the 1987 NCAA Division I-AA national championship.

"Every minute of every day - wins or losses, successes or failures, life or death – it all starts and ends with mastering the Little Things."
~ J.B. Grimes

J.B. Grimes was wise well beyond his years. Little did we know at the time that he wasn't just teaching us how to become great offensive linemen; his relentless pursuit of excellence in the details was one of the most important lessons for life and business we would ever learn.

Why was J.B. obsessed with inches when the football field is 300 feet long? He correctly understood that football is just like every other endeavor in life: the chasm between success and failure is infinitely deep, but only inches wide. That's why every inch matters. The only way to land on the success side of the chasm is to pay attention to every inch along the way.

I can hear the senior executives now: "I'm a big-picture guy. I have people who take care of the details." In my mind, that's a great way to fail. The big picture is comprised of tiny details. How many huge games have hinged on the offense's ability to move the football just a few inches on an extremely important play? How many potential touchdown passes were thrown just an inch too high for the receiver to reach? How many field goal attempts missed by just a few inches? There are enough missed-it-by-an-inch episodes in every football season to fill hours of film. On any given Sunday, as the saying goes, a team is just inches away from the upset of the century or a victory for the ages.

I've been fortunate enough to be associated with a number of very successful organizations, in sports and in business, and they all have one thing in common: top organizations focus intensely on executing the details flawlessly. This relentless drive to get the details absolutely correct – to cover the last few inches between failure and success - is what separates champions from everyone else. Done right, the details resonate throughout all aspects of an organization, top to bottom.

There's an extremely important caveat to keep in mind, however: you must focus on the *right* details. As an offensive lineman, the important details relate to body position, balance, movement, quickness, and blocking technique – what Coach Grimes calls the "how" of playing offensive line. Focusing on anything else is a waste of time.

No matter what business you're in, the details that matter are the ones that win customers and keep them happy. The important Little Things are the ones that attract and keep the best people. Everything else is a distraction.

Champions don't let the Little Things fall through the cracks, and the only way to achieve excellence in the Little Things is to practice them – the right ones - every day. The reality is that if JB Grimes hadn't made us exercise the fundamentals every day during football practice, we never would have become the best offensive line in college football. Strict focus on the Little Things will ensure that you stay sharp in all aspects in the game of business and life.

I'm not suggesting that by becoming excellent at the Little Things you'll experience nothing but smooth sailing. You probably won't. Just like the painful, eye-opening hit I received on my first day of football practice, life is full of haymakers, and more than a few of them are going to catch you square on the chin. Business is not easy, and "hits" will come your way in the form of lawsuits, lost accounts, missed opportunities, product recalls, bad press, and the like. Some of these hits are going to be big enough that they might even threaten to take you out of the game altogether.

But the beauty of the Little Things is that repetition builds retention. If you are constantly focused on the foundation of your business, day in and day out, and you have a laser focus on the fundamentals required to be successful, then you will have ingrained excellence into your consciousness. The hits will undoubtedly come your way, but you will be far better prepared than most, and you will be able to rely on the rock-solid fundamentals you've cultivated to see you through. You'll be less prone to making costly mistakes in disorienting situations, and you'll be far more likely to come out ahead when "all hell breaks loose," as Coach Grimes says.

Here's a short list of fundamental "Little Things" in business that sometimes slip. It's by no means all-encompassing, but it's a great starting point.

- Listen. Most people listen only closely enough to formulate their next response, which is a great way to argue, but a terrible way to understand. Champions listen with the intention of fully comprehending, and resist the temptation to focus on coming up with an immediate counter-argument. Ask clarifying questions while you're listening, summarize what you've heard, and ask the speaker to correct you if you've misunderstood.
- Pay attention. It's easy to sleepwalk through your day taking little notice of the environment around you, becoming inured to the flaws in your business that might be driving your customers away. Approach your day with a curious mind, and the details that escaped you previously will suddenly scream for your attention.
- Write it down. Even if you have a terrific memory, it isn't

good enough for the kind of perfection you're aiming to achieve. Take notes as you go about your day, make lists of Little Things that need your attention, and refer frequently to your notes. You'll be amazed at how your productivity and sharpness skyrocket.

- Read the entire contract. Judging by the length of the legal mumbo-jumbo that accompanies any product or service for sale today, it's painfully obvious that we live in a litigious society. But the truth is, given that we live in a lawsuit-happy society, you need to protect yourself and your championship business by reading all of the fine print, in every contract you sign – from everything to copier maintenance contracts to multi-billion dollar deals.

- Spend time working on your business relationships. Championship businesses are built one relationship at a time, and taking the time to cultivate effective relationships is a stupendously important Little Thing. Write thank-you notes – by hand - to vendors, customers, and employees who go above and beyond your expectations. Call your clients out of the blue and ask whether there's anything about your product or service that you can improve. Return correspondence in a timely fashion, and take just a little bit more time to make sure the tone of your reply is friendly and personable rather than "just the facts." Send gifts commemorating important events in the lives of your team members and clients, and publicly recognize your star performers. The list of ways to cultivate great professional relationships is nearly endless, and your investment in the relationships that matter to your business will reap gigantic rewards.

- Wherever you are, be fully present. Don't take your smart phone or tablet into meetings with you, and don't scroll through emails while talking to people. Honor your employees and clients with your full, undivided attention.

Avoid the urge to multi-task – no matter who you are, your mind wasn't built to ponder more than one thing at once, period. You're at your best when you give your full attention to what you're doing. There's a corollary law that's worth heeding as well: if what you're doing right now isn't important enough for your full attention, then you shouldn't be doing it in the first place.

- Be courteous. Smile. Make eye contact. Treat everyone in your organization with equal respect and dignity, regardless of the role they're playing in your business.

- Set daily goals. A friend of mine likes to say that true progress only comes about when we allow ourselves to entertain absurd ambitions, and you should write your ambitions down on paper as they occur to you. Keep a separate list for big goals, and record your daily goals – what you hope to have accomplished before you turn out the lights for the night – in a prominent place that you see frequently. Be sure to include your personal goals in this list as well, such as fitness or workout goals, relationship goals, and personal development objectives.

- Take your vacations, and make your employees take all of their vacation time. Vacations prevent burnout, stress, depression, and loss of productivity. Life is too short to put off having amazing times with your family in beautiful places on the globe.

"What you can do tomorrow, do today. What you can do today, do NOW!"
~ J.B. Grimes

Building a championship team in business means much more than having an airtight business plan. A championship team has a nearly obsessive focus on the details that matter, and champions ignore distractions. Taking the time to practice the details leads to a discipline that will spread to the rest of your organization. If your team needs more focus on the Little Things, my suggestion is to follow the example set by one of the best football coaches I've ever known: hang a giant sign in your office reminding you and your team of the importance of "THE LITTLE THINGS" and, underneath it, make a list of all the areas in your business that need a bit more attention.

Remember, champions stay focused on the Little Things. Like football, business is a game of inches, and the only way to bridge the inches-wide chasm between success and failure is to become excellent – the best in your field – at flawlessly executing the important details. Build the Little Things into every part of your daily business activity, and you're sure to build a championship organization.

Team WORKS! – Chapter 3

Master Yourself

The door to success opens inward.

Remember my embarrassing first day as a Tampa Bay Buccaneer, when I misunderstood Coach Gruden's instructions, flattened Warren Sapp, and ended up running for my life as Sapp tried to kill me with my own helmet? In the history of bonehead mistakes, that was a pretty big one. While it certainly didn't endear me to Warren or establish me as a fixture on the Buccaneer roster, the episode did serve a very important purpose in my life. The Sapp incident illustrated an imperative that now forms the backbone of my business philosophy: in order to master your market, you must first master yourself.

As I made my way from Dallas to Tampa on that fateful day in 2002, I spent the entire time converting my hopes for the future into emotional energy. That energy had no productive outlet, and only served to make me more anxious and keyed up. The more I felt the butterflies in my stomach, the more I was reminded of why I had those butterflies in the first place: my NFL career had been resuscitated, but I now had to prove my worth to a team that was poised to make a run at the title. I had a daunting task ahead of me, and while I was excited for the new opportunity, my anxious thoughts repeated themselves in a vicious self-reinforcing cycle.

This undisciplined thought process continued all through the night, robbing me of the opportunity for some precious sleep in advance of my important first day of practice as a Tampa Bay Buccaneer. I stayed up all night working myself into a lather, oscillating between excitement and nervousness and adding self-imposed pressure to what was already a stressful situation. My thoughts kept returning to my burning desire to make a strong first impression on my new teammates and coaches, and I kept ruminating on the enormity of the opportunity. Instead of sleeping, I wore a hole in the hotel room carpet by pacing back and forth, thinking about all the different ways I needed to excel in the coming hours in order to prove my mettle.

I was elated, excited, and nervous, and while I knew that my nervous energy was actually reducing my chances of making a positive first impression in Tampa, I lacked the maturity and self-mastery to stop the destructive emotional cycle. There were two key aspects of controlling my mental landscape that I didn't understand.

"Rule your mind or it will rule you."
~ *Horace*

First, all of my unproductive emotional energy arose from my focus on the past and the future, instead of the present moment. In the recent past, I had been released from two different teams in two consecutive years, which certainly isn't the kind of track record I had hoped to put together in the early part of my professional football career. As I dwelled on my recent NFL history, I continued to add self-inflicted pressure to turn that record around and make a name for myself in Tampa. Making the roster on an NFL team brings plenty of pressure in and of itself, and there is absolutely no need to add any unnecessary stress! The energy I devoted to getting worked up over past mistakes and missed opportunities was definitely not productive energy. It contributed to my nervousness, and depleted my confidence going into my next opportunity.

I was also spending a great deal of time looking forward into the future, trying to imagine all of the scenarios I might face and devise the best approach to conquer the challenges in each of them. This might sound like I was "preparing" for the upcoming test, but the reality is that I was doing the precise opposite. I was *already* prepared, in great physical shape and ready to go, and I should have just trusted in my skills and my work ethic. Instead, the time I spent trying to predict what the future might hold just conjured even more anxiety and stress.

You might ask, "But doesn't being prepared mean that you

think through all of the likely scenarios that you'll encounter?" Absolutely, with an extremely important caveat: you should only spend time thinking about possible future scenarios if you can influence their outcome through concrete action *right now*. Devising a solid plan for a possible future scenario is one thing, but no amount of prior pondering in the middle of the night was ever going to help me have quicker feet, stronger leg drive, and better arm strength to make my blocks effectively. No amount of nocturnal cogitation was going to give me greater skill, endurance, or mental toughness to help me convince my coaches that they had made a great investment by signing me. I hadn't yet been issued a Buccaneer playbook, so it's not like I was up all night learning the offense and studying plays (though I don't know anyone who advocates pulling an all-nighter to "study" for an athletic event). My thoughts about the future were serving absolutely no useful purpose. Worse, not only was my nervous thinking not useful, it was extremely detrimental, causing me to show up for my first day as a Buccaneer tired and strung out on adrenaline.

Instead of wasting mental energy by revisiting the past and worrying about the future, I would have been much better off if I had just focused entirely on *right now*. The past only exists in our memory, and the future only exists in our imagination, but the present moment is *real*. In fact, because future and past only exist in our heads, you might argue that the present moment – right now – is the only real thing we ever have. It is the only space in which we can directly influence the quality of our lives and the quality of our efforts aimed at reaching our goals.

With less than half a day's notice before I needed to show up and impress the Tampa Bay Buccaneers, there is only one thing I had the power to do that would have improved my odds at making a splash (and I mean a slightly more positive splash than the kind that makes Warren Sapp want to end your life!). I had the power to show up rested and relaxed. Instead of showing up stressed out and strung out, I could have begun my first practice calm and confident.

How would that have helped? It's simple: the people who perform best under pressure are the ones who most successfully *ignore* the pressure. They remain calm and in full control of their faculties while others around them go a little bit crazy. Champions have confidence in their preparation, and believe they have the skill and wherewithal to handle any situation that might arise. This mindset has the amazing result of actually making them better at dealing with difficult situations. Not worrying about the outcome produces better outcomes!

Champions also embrace the reality that there will be times when their efforts fall short of their goals and expectations, *and they don't waste a nanosecond worrying about it before the fact.* Occasional failures are a fact of life for everyone. Failure is the price of admission to sports, business, and everything else worthwhile, and champions don't ever let worries about future situations cloud their thinking right now.

"I think the guys who best control their emotions are going to win."
~ Tiger Woods

The second major tenet of self-mastery that I failed to use to my advantage during the Sapp incident is the simple fact that we have the power to choose the thoughts we think. Many of us feel that our thoughts just happen to us, as if they're something external like rain showers or stubbed toes, but champions understand that they have both the privilege and the responsibility of choosing the thoughts they think.

Our thoughts are the fuel that drives the engine of our entire lives. Our thoughts can instantly determine our internal biochemistry - in my case, during the night prior to my first day in Tampa, my thoughts caused gallons of adrenaline and cortisol, a stress hormone, to course through my veins and exhaust my muscle cells. The "fight or flight" response kept me from sleeping, which is detrimental because the body cleans house and removes many toxins from inside our cells only when we're asleep, so my all-night rumination was a double-whammy. Just by what I chose to think, I doomed myself to showing up for practice with a cloudy head and a tired body. Every cell in my body suffered from my choice of thoughts.

My state of mind didn't just rob me of rest. It was also the root cause of my buffoonery during my first practice as a Buc. I allowed myself to become so emotional and wound up that I wasn't able to think clearly, and I was so trapped inside my own head that I missed a number of important cues that would have told me that we were doing a walk-through drill, and not a full-contact exercise. The repetitive, high-pressure, high-emotion thoughts that were zinging around in my brain absolutely blinded me to the important details.

It may seem ironic that my extreme desire to perform well is precisely the reason I didn't perform well, but it turns out that this is how things work for most people. It's a normal human phenomenon, but it doesn't mean we're doomed to poor performance due to excess nervous energy. We have the power to choose calmness and confidence in any situation, and that's exactly what champions do.

Our thoughts also have a more long-term impact. They directly shape the external circumstances around us, because our thoughts determine our actions, and over time, our actions determine what we make of ourselves and of the opportunities we encounter in life.

"As a man thinks, so he is."
~ *James Allen*

As we saw in Chapter 2, high achievement in both athletics and business requires years of daily dedication to doing the Little Things that bridge the inches-wide gap between success and failure. You're not always going to feel motivated to do those things. But if you have made the choice to become excellent in your chosen field, you will also make the daily choice to do what's necessary. You may not always enjoy everything that building championship-caliber skills requires, but you will certainly enjoy the improvement you notice in yourself and in your results.

Having the right mindset shapes not only what you do with your time, but also how you do it. There is a fundamental truth that you bring the quality to any activity you undertake, not the other way around. Another way of saying this is that you get out what you put in – put in the effort, hours, and mental energy, and you'll not only achieve great results on the given task, but you'll also achieve significant growth as a result of the process. You'll learn new skills and discover new details about the way your business and industry work.

On a major college or professional football team, players are expected to put in the appropriate time in the weight room to get stronger, faster, and quicker. But we all know that just showing up in the weight room doesn't do a thing for us. It's the quality of our workout – which comes directly from the quantity of our effort and the quality of each movement we perform – that garners positive results. Our level of effort correlates directly to the quality of our mindset. True dedication isn't reflected in just driving to the gym, but in paying the price in sweat and blood to become a truly world-class athlete, and that requires a champion's mental discipline.

The same phenomenon is true in a business environment as well. Let's say that you're faced with a fairly menial task, such as drafting a policy message for one of your divisions. Playing wordsmith for a memo is probably not something you ever envisioned as a key part of your path to business greatness, and it might be tempting to blaze through it as quickly as possible so you can get on to more important matters. But that might be a mistake. Drafting the policy memo is an opportunity in disguise, and spending the time to get it right might have the important side effect of providing you with greater insight into the way your business works. If you take the time to fully understand the issue at hand, you'll also have a far better understanding of your business overall.

"Who are you kidding?" you might be asking. "One well-written policy memo doesn't make a championship business leader." You're absolutely right, just like one great workout doesn't make an NFL superstar. But it's the commitment to approaching every task with the same dedication to excellence and the same intention to achieve greatness that catapults you ahead of your peers and competitors. Your efforts compound over time, and your investment in doing the Little Things right – all the time, every time - sows seeds of greatness in each corner of your business. They won't all sprout into lucrative, world-beating ventures. But enough of them will take root to propel you toward your goals.

"Mastery of others is strength. Mastery of yourself is true power."
~ Lao Tzu

What I've described above is the essence of mental toughness. It's the strength and discipline to dedicate yourself to the pursuit of excellence on a daily basis, and it's the even greater strength and self-control required to control your mindset in tough situations so that you can perform at your best. Champions know that mental toughness is nothing more than exerting control over your thoughts.

So, given that your thoughts determine your success, how do you gain control over the thoughts in your head? Do you need to spend hours sitting in the lotus position with your palms up and your eyes closed, pondering the "suchness" of existence? If that works for you, knock yourself out, but it's not necessary in order to make the kind of positive changes that will vault you over the success bar. There are a couple of tricks you can use to become conscious of the prevailing attitudes and habitual thought patterns that run around inside your brain every day, and to turn around any negativity that might be sabotaging your efforts.

I call the first trick the "King for a Nanosecond" technique. When a situation arises that provokes a strong emotional reaction, particularly one that might tempt me to get angry, I use this technique. It's a two-step process. First, I remind myself that I have both the power and the responsibility to choose how I react to every given situation. This usually takes a lot of the steam out of the initial flood of emotion, and prevents me from saying or doing something impulsive that I will later regret.

The second step is where the "King for a Nanosecond" idea comes in. I imagine that I'm the king of my own kingdom, able to choose the outcomes that I want, and then I ask myself, "What outcome do I want for this situation?" For example, on the gridiron, I may want to recover quickly from a holding penalty or missed block and return to top form on the very next play. In business, I may want a tense discussion with a client to end in a friendly and lucrative agreement. Or I may want a team member to bounce back quickly from a significant setback or costly mistake. Once I decide on the result I want for the emotionally charged situation, it's much easier to set the anger or disappointment aside and choose the action that best moves the situation toward my desired outcome.

"Mental toughness is a state of mind. You might call it 'character in action.'"
~ Vince Lombardi

What do I mean by that? Each of the example situations above has presented me with a decision, and my choice in the moment of decision largely determines the situation's outcome. Depending on my actions, things could resolve nicely, moving me further toward my goals, or the situation could devolve into a heated, emotional, and counterproductive mess. I could berate myself for the penalty or missed block, and I could get angry at the client or my employee, but what purpose would it serve? Would my anger produce better performance with fewer mental errors on the next play? Would an angry response produce a signed deal with the client? A sharper employee? In most cases, the answer is a resounding "no," as an angry, emotional reaction rarely results in a positive outcome. By quietly and quickly reminding myself that the results I desire aren't usually attainable through emotional outbursts, I am able to regain my wits and use the situation to my advantage. Taking a step back from the emotion in my role as the "king" allows me to view things strategically, and reminds me to align my immediate thoughts and actions with my goals.

The same technique works when I don't feel like accomplishing what I call my "dues-paying" activities, or those things that aren't necessarily enjoyable or glamorous, but that are necessary to build my championship business. I apply the same mental discipline that got me into the gym as a professional athlete on those days when I would rather do anything else. I take a quick step back from the current feeling – in this case laziness or weariness – and ask myself about what I want in the long run. This refocusing effort pays huge dividends, as it helps me view the current task, which might seem unpleasant at the moment, in its proper place in the bigger picture: as a necessary step toward my long-term objectives. Suddenly, the task takes on a new quality. Or, more accurately, I bring a new quality to the task – instead of viewing it as just another chore, I begin to view the work as a valuable step that's in line with my life's goals, and

I devote far more effort and energy to it than I ever would have without this critical shift in my mindset.

Self-mastery doesn't just involve the discipline to do the things you should do. Mastering yourself also requires you to stop yourself from doing the things you *shouldn't* do! My good friend Roman Oben is a terrific example of this kind of discipline. Roman enjoyed an incredible twelve-year career as a highly respected offensive lineman, and was a member of the 2002 Tampa Bay team that won the Super Bowl. In a league where over 75% of players find themselves either bankrupt or in severe financial distress within two years after retirement, due mostly to living a horribly undisciplined financial life while the big NFL paychecks roll in, Roman was the picture of self-restraint. "I didn't have 20 gold chains and 15 cars," he says. "I had a '96 Land Cruiser with 60,000 miles on it."

Instead of partying like a rock star, Roman spent his offseason time earning a Master's degree and serving as an intern for two members of Congress. Roman didn't blow his cash on bar tabs and Bentleys, and he didn't waste his talent by frittering away his offseason time. He thought strategically about his life goals, and he used those strategic thoughts to help him make terrific personal decisions – even while the vast majority of his friends and peers were busy doing the precise opposite. After his years of NFL stardom ended, Roman's disciplined personal life left him with his family and finances intact, and gave him tremendous tools to launch his post-NFL business career.

Mental toughness is all about rooting out and eliminating negativity and counterproductive thoughts and emotions. Often the most damaging thought patterns are sneakier and less obvious than the others, though, and eliminating those "success saboteurs" requires a bit more awareness.

Fortunately, you have a built-in negative thought detector: your body. Your body will always tell you if you're feeling stress.

That's useful, because I've found that stress is often related to fears of inadequate preparation, which can be a terrific clue to point you to the area of your business that needs more of your attention.

Just like the "King for a Nanosecond" technique, mastering this stress to get yourself back in championship form is a two-step process. Step one is to take a second to figure out if your body feels tense anywhere. I'm not saying you need to put on spa music and burn incense in your office, or retreat to a dark room and lie down. You just need to take a quick second to see if any part of your body feels uptight. Most of the time, your physical tension will go away as soon as you become aware of it, and your body will instantly and automatically relax. Step two is to be honest with yourself about why you're feeling uptight. You'll be surprised what you learn.

Why bother with this? For one very important reason: it's easy to lie to yourself about what you're really thinking, but your body always tells the truth. You might be consciously trying to repeat positive thoughts, but a tense body tells you that you're really feeling something quite opposite from the positive outlook you're trying to foster. Usually, it doesn't take long to figure out the source of the tension. Once you discover what's causing your worry and anxiety, you'll be able to do something about it.

"Leaders are made, they are not born. They are made by hard effort, which is the price which all of us must pay to achieve any goal that is worthwhile."
~ Vince Lombardi

Here's an example. When I spent the entire trip from Dallas to Tampa getting anxious and keyed up, part of the issue was a powerful feedback cycle between the body and brain. When we think stressful thoughts, our body reacts by becoming tense. Our muscles contract and we feel the adrenaline in our gut. The body reports these sensations back to the brain, which interprets them for what they are: evidence of stress. This perpetuates the stressed-out mindset that brought on the tense and nervous feelings in the first place, creating another vicious cycle.

In order to become aware of those sensations, we have to first take a step back from them. This has the effect of immediately reducing their intensity (don't believe me? Try it!), and it gives us the opportunity to discover their root cause – which is Step Two. In my case before my first practice in Tampa, all the nervous energy had a very simple explanation. I was excited for my new opportunity as a Tampa Bay Buccaneer, but I was also concerned that I wouldn't be up to the task, and that I wouldn't make a strong enough first impression to earn a more permanent spot on the roster.

If I had it to do over again, I would apply the two-step process to mastering my nervous energy. I would first recognize the tension running around in my body and take a step back from it. It would have instantly diminished in intensity. I would then quietly ask myself what I was worried about. I've learned that the answer would have come fairly quickly, and I would have been able to address the root cause of my worry.

Armed with this knowledge, I could have easily stopped the cycle of destructive thoughts and exhausting emotions. I could have acknowledged that things weren't guaranteed to go exactly as I wanted them to go, and rather than spending energy worrying about what might happen, I could have simply committed myself to giving all of the effort I was capable of giving and letting the chips fall where they may. I could have decided to place my confidence in my years of preparation, and trust that if my absolute best effort didn't result in a Hall-of-Fame career as a Buccaneer, it just wasn't meant to be. This would have broken the destructive emotional cycle and put me in the right frame of mind to pour everything out on the field as I pursued my dream, but not mentally sabotage my chances at success by becoming overly emotional and blinded by adrenaline.

"Competing is exciting and winning is exhilarating, but the true prize will always be the self-knowledge and understanding that you have gained along the way."
~ *Sebastian Coe, four-time Olympic medalist*

Occasionally, the two-step process of figuring out whether there are negative thoughts floating around, and then identifying what might be causing those thoughts, will reveal an aspect of my life or business that needs attention. If I feel my gut tense up when I think about an upcoming meeting, event, or client pitch, I pause to figure out why. Sometimes it's due to a contentious relationship that needs some work to smooth over, and other times it's because I feel underprepared in a particular area. Taking a quick second to inventory my thoughts often points me in the right direction to keep moving forward toward my goals, and deal head-on with any issues that might be lurking or lingering.

Mastering your emotions and your thoughts – the very definition of mental toughness - is an essential element of becoming a champion business leader. Because your thoughts determine the quality of your entire life, and can either ensure your success or prevent it entirely, it pays to spend the minimal effort necessary to get a handle on the kinds of thoughts you allow to float around in your mind. If you find yourself ruminating on past failures or worrying about what might happen in the future, simply knock it off. Instead, ask yourself what you can do *right now*, in this moment, to propel you toward your goals. If you run into an emotionally charged situation, play "King for a Nanosecond" and decide the outcome you'd prefer most, then take the strategic course of action with the highest probability of producing that outcome you want. Last, take just a second several times a day to figure out whether you're carrying tension, and to discover what negative thoughts are behind that unease. Those thoughts will point you either to pointless fears that you can eradicate by focusing on the things that you can control, or they'll help you identify aspects of your business that need more work. Once you master these extremely simple but exceptionally powerful techniques, you'll be infinitely more effective as the leader of your championship business team.

PART 2

THE TEAM

Team WORKS! – Chapter 4

Assembling Your Championship Team

Marquee players don't usually make championship teams.
But championship teams make marquee players!

"The classic problem with entrepreneurs is that they have a hard time delegating. But that's really crazy. Recruiting other executives is critical, so is dealing with customers and dealing with regulators. Those are functions that only the top founders can do."
~ *Robert Pozen*

You've worked hard to improve yourself, and you've come a long way in your development as the future leader of a championship business team. You've clearly defined your role as a player-coach, responsible not only for getting the job done as the key player on the field, but also responsible for setting the strategic direction and making intelligent game-time decisions as well. You've established a deliberate plan of attack to master the details, the life-blood of your business, and you've taken on a nearly-fanatical respect for the value of the Little Things. You've also done the hard work of mastering your emotional life to serve rather than squash your success.

Now what?

Business is a team sport, and this is a book about building a championship business team. Now that we've covered the necessary personal development areas that will make you into a championship player-coach, it's time to focus on how to pick the all-star players who will form the backbone of the team that takes you to the top of your industry.

In their own words: Super Bowl Champion Offensive Lineman Roman Oben

Many critics argue that Jon Gruden won Super Bowl XXXVII with a team he inherited from Tony Dungy. That is partially true, as the defensive team stayed intact from the prior season. But Jon Gruden's offensive overhaul made the difference in what we were able to accomplish that earlier incarnations of our offense hadn't been able to achieve. Jon built the right offensive team to achieve our championship goals.

In the entire history of the franchise, the Tampa Bay Buccaneers hadn't won a game when the weather was below 40 degrees. My theory on this dismal record was that from high school to college, many of the players drafted by the Buccaneers had never left the state of Florida or the southeastern region of the United States, resulting in an inability to perform efficiently in cold-weather climates. The same theory holds true for teams that play their home games in a dome and then have to play on the road during playoffs. This problem plagued some of Dungy's Colts teams during several postseason appearances until they were finally able to get over the hump in 2006.

Changing the organizational culture *was the biggest reason our 2002 Bucs team was able to bring home a championship. I realized that Coach Gruden had brought in many of our new offensive players, including myself, from other NFL franchises in colder cities during the prior season. I think Gruden did that on purpose. He knew that the road to a championship was bound to take the team through a number of cold-weather markets during playoff season.*

Instead of just picking the best players available, Coach Gruden picked the **right** *players for his team – ones with the right experience and background to help his team get to the next level.*

The new offensive players also challenged the defense every day in practice, as many of the new players weren't intimidated by the panache and reputation of our defensive stars at the time, including Derrick Brooks, Warren Sapp, Simeon Rice, John Lynch, Ronde Barber, and others.

By the time we got to the NFC Championship game against the Philadelphia Eagles, our offensive culture was completely different than during the year prior. We were ready to attack the Eagles on their own turf. They had beaten us earlier in the season, and we were hungry for revenge. Our new offensive team culture of *toughness and efficiency helped us carry the day despite the notorious Philadelphia cold. Jon Gruden's group of the **right** players went on to beat the Raiders in the Super Bowl, a dream come true for me and my teammates.*

Roman Oben is a 12-year NFL veteran and Super Bowl Champion Offensive Lineman. Since his retirement in 2008, he is a sports Broadcaster and public speaker in the New York City area as well as managing partner of Fusion Sports Group.

I'll warn you in advance that I'm not going to spill all of the beans in this chapter. I'm going to save one tiny little item for later. Actually, it's not a small item at all – it's the magic ingredient, the silver bullet, the sorcerer's stone, the essential element of a championship team. That one thing is the glue that will hold everything else together. This chapter is about the "everything else" that goes in to constructing your championship team in business.

I'm going to give you a number of winning attributes that your team members absolutely must have, if you're going to have any hope of forming a championship business team. It's important to keep in mind as you read this chapter that the attributes I'm about to spell out for you will be necessary, *but not sufficient*, for your team's success. You won't succeed without a team comprised of power-players who, collectively and individually, possess these killer qualities in spades. But even if you find players with all of the attributes I'm about to mention, it's entirely possible for you to assemble a team full of talented all-stars that goes absolutely nowhere. Regardless of how many other qualities your team members have going for them, your team will flop unless it's held together by the Secret Ingredient. I'll fill you in on that all-important magic elixir soon enough, but first, let's explore some of the nuts and bolts – the Little Things – of business acumen.

No matter what business you're in, the currency of your business is information. Customers may vaguely or even acutely sense that they have a need or a pain point, but they have no idea that your killer product or service can meet their needs or alleviate their pain unless you successfully and compellingly communicate your value proposition – which is nothing more than information about your business and its potential benefits to your customers. This central truth is a clue to the first attribute I look for in a potential business team member: clear, concise, correct, calm, cool, and collected communication skills.

Really? The 300-lb offensive lineman who used to make his living smashing his skull into other 300-lb behemoths values something as touchy-feely as *communication skills* at the top of his list of essential bread-and-butter business team attributes (after the Secret Ingredient, that is)?

Absolutely. Business runs on the flow of information, and information only moves through communication. We're after what Aristotle described as the art of "discovering all available means of persuasion in a given instance." Aristotle was referring to the ability to make clear, cogent connections between salient points in order to compose a compelling argument to win over an audience, which is the precise skill your team needs to master in order to close sales and generate revenue for your business.

A great football team is also highly skilled in the art of transferring vast amounts of information quickly and clearly among teammates. The offensive line is a critical communication hub for the team, and there is an enormous amount of information flowing between linemen down in the trenches of an NFL line of scrimmage. Most people think it's just the quarterback who calls the signals before every offensive play, and it's true that he's responsible for making sure the play meets the coach's intent in light of any last-second changes the defensive team may throw at the offense, but there's just as much communication going on between the offensive linemen. In fact, on a good football team, communication usually works from the inside out. It starts with the center and spreads to the guards, tackles and tight ends, who pass signals to the receivers. All of this happens in just a couple of seconds.

Each "audible," or change in plan ordered by the quarterback just seconds prior to the start of the play, has a ripple effect throughout the offensive line. A minor change in the play might mean that each lineman is now responsible for an entirely different blocking pattern. A major change may mean that instead of shooting forward to block the nearest defender out of the way of the running back, who's rushing headlong toward the line of scrimmage in order to move the ball forward on the ground, the lineman instead has to stand his ground and stop the onrushing defenders from reaching the quarterback before he's able to throw a pass downfield to a receiver.

Because the environment is so dynamic, communication is critically important. Can you imagine what happens when one half of the line has the wrong idea about what the quarterback wants for the play? Complete bedlam. Miscommunications frequently result in plays that are terrible enough to be immortalized on the blooper reel.

Adding to the complexity is the inconvenient fact that the defensive players don't sit cooperatively still while the offensive line figures out what to do. While the offensive team is required to remain perfectly still before the start of the play, defenders are bound by no such inconvenience. As long as they stay on their side of the ball, opposite the offensive team, defenders are allowed to move around as much as they want. This means that offensive linemen need to communicate extremely quickly and clearly about their blocking assignments in order to prevent a wily defender from sneaking through and ruining the play. It's easier said than done, and mistakes happen frequently, but championship teams reduce the number of missed assignments to the absolute minimum through extremely disciplined and well-rehearsed communication skills.

The same phenomenon happens in business as well. The dynamic business environment demands that your championship team make adjustments on the fly, and doing so effectively requires excellent communication skills. In order to prevent missed assignments and disastrous outcomes, your team's internal communication needs to be airtight.

Because your business operates in a competitive environment, your communication also needs to be secure. In football, the defense can quickly pick up on predictable forms of communication. If the center constantly calls "rover" and then proceeds with a zone blocking pattern to the right side, a good defense will quickly decipher the code word and negate any advantage gained by the audible. You want to recruit people who have the disciplined communication habits and situational awareness to keep your trade secrets from your competitors.

"Sometimes, to ensure that a talented individual will work for you, or will stay working with you, you need to be flexible. Money is not always the great motivator here. Talented people want a good salary, of course, but surprisingly often they are more attracted to new opportunities and challenges."
~ Felix Dennis

External communication skills are even more important, because the way your team members communicate to the outside world directly influences the number of dollars that flow into your business. Clearly, effective communication skills are a non-negotiable asset that your hires must possess.

When you're recruiting new team members, pay close

attention to their mannerisms, the clarity of their speech, and their non-verbal communication habits. Imagine your hopeful hires standing in front of line-of-business executives in your client companies. Are you certain your prospective players will be effective proselytes for the better mousetrap your business builds? Will they stand confidently and deliver clear, concise, effective presentations? Will they respond thoughtfully but quickly to questions? Do they exude competence and confidence? Do they have that certain *gravitas* that makes people take notice even before your prospects open their mouth to speak? If you can't easily imagine your prospective team members absolutely hitting it out of the park in front of your clients, you need to keep looking. In order to build a championship team, you'll need players in every major functional area of your business who have these kinds of professional communication skills in abundance.

Of course, there's always room to improve communication techniques, and we'll talk about the most effective ways to do just that in Chapters 6 and 7. But you just can't teach the intangibles. A firm handshake, a steady, friendly gaze, a ready smile and comfortable laugh, intelligent and engaging conversation, and an attentive (but not obsequious) ear are the basic attributes that any quality hire will bring with them as they darken your door for the first time. There just isn't time or money enough to develop those basic qualities in your team members if they don't already possess them on day one. So if you haven't yet found team members like that, there's only one option: keep looking. Your championship team needs championship communicators.

> *"Development can help great people be even better—but if I had a dollar to spend, I'd spend 70 cents getting the right person in the door."*
> *~ Paul Russell*

That brings us to another important point: the backbone of

successful communication is, well, backbone! Many business situations require your team members to stand their ground on important issues, sometimes with powerful people applying great pressure in the opposite direction. Each of your championship players needs the intestinal fortitude to stand up to the pressures of negotiating with potential clients, vendors, and other new hires.

How can you tell whether a prospective player has this kind of nerve? The nonverbal communication habits we discussed earlier (friendly but unwavering eye contact, a firm handshake, a calm demeanor under pressure, etc.) are a terrific starting point, as these communication skills usually belong to people who have a strong sense of self-respect. Why is self-respect important? I view it as the backbone of backbone! You can't stand up under pressure if you don't know in your heart that you're valuable, worthwhile, prepared, and effective.

In football, this kind of pressurized communication takes the form of a longstanding gridiron tradition: "trash talk." "Talking trash" is the art and science of getting inside your opponent's head, with the goal of making him doubt, if ever so slightly, whether or not he's up to the challenge of defeating you on any given play. Vicious and funny by turns, trash talking is a part of the game that few fans are privileged to experience or even know about, but suffice it to say that no part of a player's appearance, skill, life, or ancestry are off limits. Good trash talking often causes opposing players to make costly and embarrassing mental errors – which are fodder for even more trash talk.

Clearly, verbal mud-slinging doesn't make much sense in a business environment. It's a great way to alienate everyone around you. But I bring it up here because there is only one way to withstand a withering assault of trash talk from an opponent: you must have an unwavering belief in yourself and in your abilities. Standing up to a trash-talk virtuoso, a sultan of slam, takes the same kind of backbone that your team members will need in order to stand their ground in a tough negotiation session or board meeting.

Of course, you can never be 100% certain about a person's fortitude by spending just a few minutes with them. We'll spend time in Chapters 5 and 6 describing how to make doubly sure that you've hired the right team members as you prepare them for "business battle," but there's one thing you can take to the bank: if prospective hires don't respect themselves enough to look you in the eye when they talk to you, or have the strength of character to respectfully but confidently assert an opinion that differs from yours, it's best to thank them for their time and send them on their way. There just isn't time to coddle them along while they grow healthy self-esteem.

"Talent is indispensable, although it is 'always' replaceable.
Just remember the simple rules concerning talent:
Identify It,
Hire It,
Nurture It,
Reward It,
Protect It.
And when the time comes, Fire It."
~ Felix Dennis

Successful business teams are also comprised of players with another key attribute: the fire in their belly for excellence. Building a winning business team is hard work. There will be many late nights and early mornings on the way to total domination of your corner of the market, and you'll need people who share both your vision of perfection and your dedication to achieving it. Perfection happens only rarely in business, of course, but it *never* happens for teams whose members don't share the passion for perfecting the Little Things that mean the difference between success and failure.

This doesn't mean that your team members need to have a neurotic or obsessive streak. Quite the opposite – you're looking for team members who view striving for success as a pleasurable process, and who enjoy the daily work of improving their skills and improving your business' products and services. People who love the *process* of improvement, and are not just motivated by hope for positive results that might someday come from working hard, tend to achieve far greater success in the long run than people who grind themselves down for the sake of achieving a goal. If your folks don't enjoy the daily work that's necessary in order to take each of the small, incremental steps toward excellence, you can probably expect a mutiny or two as you try to build a team that focuses relentlessly on the Little Things.

How do you know whether a prospective hire enjoys the daily work that's necessary to become excellent at the details of business, and doesn't just hope they can put up with the hard work for long enough to reach an arbitrary goal? It's impossible to tell for certain up front, but spending a bit of time with your prospective team members will give you great insight into what makes them tick. For instance, does the person keep in great physical shape? If so, the chances are good that they also enjoy the process – the effort, sweat, and soreness – that staying in shape demands. Working out regularly and consistently involves too much pain for most people to endure, but for the kind of people who have the mindset of continuous improvement through enjoyable (but strenuous) effort, keeping in great shape is just the kind of challenge they crave.

It's also helpful to ask your prospective hires about their previous job experiences. It's a standard part of any interview process, and you're certain to hear a somewhat canned answer, but you'll be listening for much more than just a litany of skills they've acquired and positions they've held. You're listening for *how* your prospective team members describe their experiences. In addition to having excellent communication and interview skills, do they describe the work they did previously – not their rewards, accolades, or pats on the back, but the actual *work* - in a way that sounds like they had fun doing it? Or do you get the impression that the long hours were just a means to an end? If the latter, it's probably best to keep looking. Championship teams play for the love of the game much more than for fame and glory, and winning players have precisely the same trait. It's just too hard to be successful any other way.

What about hiring big-name, marquee players to help get you "over the hump" to business greatness? I'm ambivalent. It's true that many championship teams included outstanding marquee players. Joe Montana and Steve Young with the 49ers, Terry Bradshaw with the Steelers, Brett Favre with the Packers, Tom Brady with the Patriots, Peyton Manning and the Colts, and the Broncos' John Elway are all great examples of championship teams and hall-of-fame players thriving together. But take a closer look: each of those hall-of-fame caliber marquee players became superstars *within the context of their championship team.*

So who made whom? Would Joe Montana have done as well without Jerry Rice, Roger Craig, Ronnie Lott, and a host of other incredible San Francisco players? Would Brett Favre have hoisted his Super Bowl trophy without amazing contributions from Reggie White, Desmond Howard, LeRoy Butler, Gilbert Brown, and Mark Chmura? Can you imagine Terry Bradshaw dominating the NFL and winning four championships without help from the Steel Curtain defense and the likes of Lynn Swann and John Stallworth on the other end of his rocket passes? It's clear that championship players are only made with a championship team surrounding them.

Don't get me wrong – Montana, Favre, and Bradshaw were absolutely incredible players. But they were each just one player among many on a championship team, and they rose to legendary status as a result of their contribution to legendary teams. They certainly earned their fame, but not in a vacuum.

History is far less kind to established marquee players who have moved to different teams after achieving stardom. Montana's foray in Kansas City and Favre's time in New York are great examples of great players who had a difficult time recreating the magic of yesteryear in a new and different team environment. Both turned in forgettable performances.

For my money, you're better off focusing on establishing a championship team culture that will form the right environment to develop your own future hall-of-famers. Marquee players often come with a hefty price tag, and they sometimes bring a bit of undesirable ego in tow as well. You might successfully recruit a world-beating salesman with a terrific track record, but if he isn't a good fit with the rest of your team, you're not likely to see an appreciable lift in your business' overall performance. Go for rock-steady team players with all of the attributes you want, and your superstars will emerge naturally over time.

There's another reason not to spend much time seeking marquee players. It's a phenomenon in today's business environment that I call the "pseudo-superstar syndrome," and it relates to the number of degrees and qualifications that many applicants feel compelled to add to their resume. I have met and interviewed dozens of would-be players for my business team who hold MBAs, PhDs, and a laundry list of other impressive academic accolades, but who have very little "real world" experience (not to mention a serious lack of interpersonal communication skills in some cases). Don't get me wrong - education is a critical component, especially in a technology-driven market, and there are certainly career environments that are more conducive to certain personality traits, but I would argue that the pendulum has swung way too far. We tend to overvalue educational qualifications at the expense of meaningful business experience. I've seen many applicants who literally have the best looking resume that money can buy (student loan money, that is), but these pseudo-superstars lack the experience and basic communication skills to contribute meaningfully in a fast-paced business environment.

There is a huge difference between a perfect resume (degrees, the "right" jobs, awards, etc.) and a perfect candidate – one who has terrific communication skills, intangibles, backbone, and the fire in his belly to become excellent at the Little Things. It isn't even a contest - I instantly choose the person with a firm grip and steady eye contact over the "paper tiger" with the impressive-sounding list of academic accolades.

I've listed a few non-negotiable attributes your new hires should have, but they're not always easy characteristics to spot right away. That's why I advocate putting together something akin to a "recruiting visit" to help you and your team get to know a prospective hire on a more in-depth level than the usual interview process allows. Major college and professional football programs host recruiting visits to allow prospective players to become familiar with the facilities, players, coaches, and local area. Many programs really roll out the red carpet for high-priority prospects in order to make the best possible impression. When Peyton Manning became available after leaving the Colts, teams fell all over themselves to impress him with private jets, local celebrities, and even a parade or two. That's a bit over the top, and counterproductive for our purposes.

I recommend giving your prospects a genuine day-in-the-life experience, prosaic as it might sound. That way you don't falsely elevate your prospect's expectations, and you'll also allow your team members to get to know hopeful hires in a less contrived environment. You'll want to neck down your list of "maybe" candidates to just a few of the strongest prospects, and bring them in for a full day or two of activities and meetings. Let them tour the facilities, sit in on actual meetings, and give your team members and department heads the chance to talk with prospects one-on-one. This gives everyone involved more opportunity to determine whether you're likely to be a good fit for each other.

Before the clock runs out on this chapter, let's recap the criteria I use to find championship teammates. Because business success demands effective information flow, don't compromise on your candidates' communication skills. Air-tight intangibles are non-negotiable, and championship teams are comprised of people who love the *process* – the daily effort – of becoming fantastic at the Little Things. Don't waste time trying to land marquee players, and avoid the "pseudo-superstar syndrome" by digging deeper to see if there's any substance behind the best resume money can buy. If you follow these guidelines, you'll be well on your way to assembling a legendary team of your own!

Team WORKS! – Chapter 5

Redshirt the Rookies

Even the best players in the world need to gain experience

When I was a high school senior in Plano, Texas, I had it all. I was an all-state and all-American athlete with more college recruiting attention than I could handle. Major college football programs all over the country courted me to join their offensive line. Every college team in the country wanted me on their squad because my size, speed, strength, and talents had separated me from my competition. I was big and bad, and I knew it!

After a great deal of deliberation, I accepted a full scholarship to Texas A&M University. As I set off from home to report to the football team and begin the grueling gridiron tradition of two-a-day practices in the summer heat, I somehow had it in my mind that I would walk onto the A&M practice field and enjoy the same level of respect and success that I had experienced in the much smaller world – with much smaller competitors - of high school football.

I was seriously wrong.

When I arrived in the Texas A&M locker room, I couldn't help but notice that every player I saw was every bit as gifted as I was. Everywhere I looked, I saw large, fast, strong, intelligent, confident football players. The veterans were light-years ahead of me in all aspects of their development. I was big, strong, and quick, but they were bigger, stronger, faster and much smarter about the game than I was.

This was a completely new situation for me. I was a tough and talented young athlete from high school, with national accolades to my credit. I was the kid who dominated my high school competition, and I was accustomed to imposing my will upon whoever was unlucky enough to line up across the line of scrimmage from me. But this was a different game entirely. Where previously I dominated, my A&M teammates dominated me. Day after day during our grueling full-contact training drills in the Texas sun, the older, more established veterans on the team absolutely crushed me. It was overwhelming, a little demoralizing, and even a bit frightening!

It wasn't just the daily beatings I took that began to weigh on me. The entire environment was new and exciting, but also strange and uncomfortable. Like most college students, my freshman year marked the first time I'd lived anywhere but under my parents' roof. When school began, I couldn't help but notice that college academics were a completely different ballgame as well. My classes were difficult, professors were demanding, and the level of effort required to succeed academically in college was well beyond what high school had demanded of me.

Everything seemed to hit me all at once. I had football, school, and a burgeoning social life, and for the first time, I had to start learning how to fend for myself away from the comforting environment of home. My entire world had changed around me in a matter of days. Becoming a Division I college athlete was an enormous step in my career and life, but it felt as if I was thrown into it like a piece of raw meat tossed into the lion's den. I felt I was the right player for the team, and I knew that I had a solid foundation for becoming a great football player, but I felt completely overwhelmed by the enormous changes I had just experienced.

In high school, a few guys were quick. In college, *everyone* was quick, and the game seemed to move twice as fast. I wasn't ready to admit this, but I just wasn't ready to jump in the mix with the established competition yet. I wasn't yet ready for what football people call the "speed of the game."

"You're young and you're strong, but you're just not ready."
~ Mike Clark, Former Texas A&M Strength and Conditioning Coach

One afternoon after the second of two particularly tough practice sessions, the head coach pulled me aside and said, "Chris, we think you are one of the best young players we've seen, and we think you have the potential to be a star at Texas A&M. But we want to make sure that you maximize your talents and develop your skills. We're going to give you an extra year to make it happen. We're going to redshirt you."

My conversation with the coach left conflicting emotions swirling around inside me. I was both happy and a little bit devastated! The coach had paid me a number of great compliments, but they were punctuated by the news that I was being redshirted, which is a college football euphemism for being placed on the bench for an **entire year**. I was crushed by the thought that I would miss out on game day fun, the chance to compete with my teammates against some of the best college football teams in the country, for my entire freshman year. What was I going to do? I wanted to play, not ride the pine!

Fortunately, what I thought was a tragedy, turned out to be a tremendous blessing. According to the rules of the National Collegiate Athletics Association, a player has only four seasons in which they're allowed to play varsity football games. This rule prevents college programs from fielding teams made up of seven-year college football veterans, which would skew competition and subject other players to greater injury risk. Playing even one play in one game cashes in the entire season's worth of a player's eligibility, and starts the four-year countdown to the end of their competition eligibility.

The NCAA offers a provision to help players develop without using up a year of eligibility. By "redshirting" a player in his first year, the NCAA does not count the year against a player's four available years of collegiate eligibility. This has the effect of granting the player a 5th year of college athletics experience. The first year, or redshirt year, is spent on the practice squad, becoming familiar with the speed of the college game, the systems, plays, and procedures that the team uses, and the workout regimen required to maintain the size, strength, and quickness needed for Division I competition.

A redshirt season gives players the ability to get accustomed to living on their own, going to school, training hard in the weight room, and practicing against the team's varsity squad. The only thing a redshirted player cannot do is play in games during their freshman year. It's a great way to gain maturity and experience – two extremely necessary ingredients for successful competition at the Division I level.

The hard part about redshirting is that it can be a serious blow to a player's ego. It was very tough for a former standout player like me to have to sit on the sidelines while my friends and teammates competed on Saturdays. My all-state and all-American accolades seemed a distant memory as I watched every game that autumn from outside the lines. I hated being a scrub freshman who wasn't allowed on the field. It was hard!

But it was crucial. My redshirt year prepared me for the extremely tough job ahead. In that first year, I trained as hard as I could. I studied the playbook as much as possible, became accustomed to the effort of earning good grades in a college academic program, and I even got acclimated to living alone. I developed strength, quickness, and disciplined footwork – all essential attributes for a successful offensive lineman. Looking back on the experience, it is clear that without the opportunity to spend a year as a redshirt freshman, I never would have had the time to develop and hone the skills that turned me into a great college football player.

"Coaches who can outline plays on a black board are a dime a dozen. The ones who win get inside their player and motivate."
~ Vince Lombardi

So how does the redshirt rule in college football relate to building a championship team in business? The answer is very simple: properly prepared players win championships and close big deals. Unprepared players get crushed. It's a no-brainer: redshirt your talent until they're ready for the speed, pressure, complexity and difficulty of game day.

If your aim is to build a championship team in business, it pays to approach your players just like the best teams in the country approach their players: championship teams invest in developing their players' talent. When you've scoured the countryside to find the most qualified people available, and you've moved mountains to hire talented players who are passionate and ready to drive the bottom line for you, you MUST respect them and their talents as an investment in your future. Your players are your lifeline and the engine of your business' success, so it's absolutely crucial to spend the resources necessary to develop their talents.

Run your own "redshirt program," of sorts. Be deliberate and disciplined about providing the right opportunities to allow your people to sufficiently develop their potential before you ask them to compete and win on game day. If you throw them in the crucible before they are ready, it's very likely they will be chewed up and spit out. But if you allow them to apply their strengths and sharpen their skills in your specific business environment, and put them in the game only after they have the necessary experience and proficiency in their role in your business, you'll set them up for fantastic success.

I sometimes hear that "real-world experience is the best teacher." That's absolutely true – and it's the best reason to establish your own redshirt program! When you redshirt your new hires, you'll be providing them the right real-world experience to be successful members of your team. But there's one important caveat: you'll give them this real-world experience in a somewhat controlled environment. You'll teach them the ropes, but they won't be exposed to high-pressure, high-stakes situations before they're ready.

Why redshirt an up-and-coming business star? The answer is simple: putting promising new hires in the game too early may expose them to situations for which they're grossly underprepared. They may shine, but they're just as likely to perform poorly, committing costly mistakes that are difficult for the rest of the team to overcome. It's far better to invest the time, money, and energy to give your future franchise players the necessary seasoning before exposing them to the bright lights of the big game.

In their own words: Legendary Hall of Fame Coach R.C. Slocum

As a coach, I had two positions on red-shirting players. First, I felt that most players needed time to acclimate to being away from home and the support group that they had enjoyed for the first 18 or so years of their lives. Freshman players are away from not only parents, but siblings, friends, pastors, coaches, etc., for the first time. For most players, the world changes overnight when they leave home and show up on campus. They live in a different city, maybe larger or smaller, but different. They have a totally different group of friends. Academics, for most, are more challenging. Certainly, football is different in terms of size, speed and competition.

The process of red-shirting, not playing in competition in the freshman year, is very helpful. It allows a young man to take a few of the challenges at a time as he moves into a new arena. One of the most important aspects is learning the expectations of the organization to which he now belongs. Coaches will be different in how they relate to the new player and will have different ways of doing things. Much like in business, the object is to understand the expectations of the "new boss" (coach) and the culture of the "new company" (team). Often, this is not easy.

From the coach's standpoint, the job is to take all these new members and sell them on becoming a team. We often referred to TEAM as an acronym for Together, Each Achieves More. This sounds simple, and it is, but it is not easily done. Each new player has his own desires and self-interests, such as how many catches he hopes to have, or how many carries, etc. However, new players' desires must be subjugated to the team's needs. They must ask themselves, what talent can I give to the team's success? We often teach that there is no I in team. Instead of I, me, and my, we wanted an atmosphere of We, Us, and Ours. Having a redshirt year is beneficial to the coach to teach these concepts and is often necessary for a young player to learn them.

That being said, I also hold a second position: There are rare individuals, I called them "difference makers," that have the ability to quickly grasp these concepts and that have the physical talent and maturity to play without the benefit of a redshirt year. These are the bright stars of the business world that "get it" right from the start. Teams and companies are made better by recognizing these person-alities and allowing them room to flourish. Maturity and experience come earlier for some than others. The challenge with the bright stars is to keep them getting better. Often, early success, before a solid foundation is laid for being a part of the team, can lead to problems. The leader, or coach, must recognize this and take steps to guarantee that this person does not undermine the overall philosophy and continuity of the team.

The real challenge for the coach, team leader, or manager, is to decide who needs more assimilation into the team and who is ready to fly.

During his 14 years as head coach, R.C. Slocum led Texas A&M to a record of 123–47–2. During his career, Slocum never had a losing season and won four conference championships. He was inducted into the College Football Hall of Fame in 2012.

Not yet convinced? It might help to know that every great player in every major sport achieved their greatness through their own personal "redshirt" program. Tiger Woods is known for his absolute domination of the professional golf tour, but his redshirt program began when he was a small child, and it consisted of hundreds of thousands – maybe even millions – of golf swings. Redshirt athletes have gone on to win national championships, Heisman trophies, and all manner of accolades.

NFL teams often do something very similar. Many teams invest heavily in players who will contribute only sparingly in their first season or two. They hire extremely talented young players, and then give them time and seasoning in a backup or special-teams role to become familiar and comfortable with the speed of the professional game. For example, college star Aaron Rodgers sat for three years as Brett Favre's backup in Green Bay, and then emerged from Favre's large shadow to become an even more effective quarterback than his legendary predecessor. Rodgers currently holds the NFL record for the best single-season and all-time quarterback rating, and has Super Bowl MVP and AP Athlete of the Year accolades to his credit.

People frequently cite Michael Jordan as an exception to the rule, as he stepped right in to basketball stardom at North Carolina. But MJ's personal redshirt experience was harsher than most: he was actually cut from his high school basketball team! Can you imagine anyone telling Michael Jordan that his basketball skills were just not quite up to par to play at the high school level? That's exactly what happened. This "redshirt opportunity in disguise" motivated him to work harder, prepare better, and, ultimately, to develop into one of the greatest talents ever to play the game. He showed up at North Carolina as what Coach Slocum calls a "difference maker" because he had already experienced all of the redshirting he needed. If it worked for MJ, it will probably work for your business too.

After you've made the decision to redshirt a new hire, it's

important to break the news of your decision in the right way. Your future superstars have likely just come from an environment in which they've performed extremely well, much like my all-American high school football experience, which means that they're probably not accustomed to sitting on the sidelines.

My Texas A&M coach's example is a great one to follow when you tell your folks that you plan to develop them further before putting them in on game day. He began the conversation by telling me how much he valued my contribution to the team, and by letting me know that he believed in me and in my talents. He told me that he thought I had a very bright future on his team, and that he was giving me a great opportunity to develop to my full potential. The encouraging way he described the redshirt opportunity left me motivated to get right to work.

> *"In sports, mental imagery is used primarily to help you get the best out of yourself in training and competition. The developing athletes who make the fastest progress and those who ultimately become their best make extensive use of mental imagery. They use it daily as a means of directing what will happen in training, and as a way of pre-experiencing their best competition performances."*
> *~ Terry Orlick*

Redshirting offered me the chance to learn all about the ins and outs of college football. It gave me the opportunity to thoroughly learn the new playbook, study my responsibilities on each play, become familiar with various tactics used by opposing defenses, analyze game footage, and much more. Redshirting gave me the opportunity to put myself in the right frame of mind in order to survive at the Division I level.

Redshirting your new hires gives you the opportunity to teach them your industry. You can teach them unique lingo, marketplace dynamics, key metrics, important vendors, key target clients, best practices in your field, your nearest competitors, and much more. Best of all, they get to learn your expectations by watching you in action as they become familiar with their new role in your company. You'll have the chance to focus their effort and develop their talent in the areas that will be most rewarding for your people and most profitable for your business.

Ideally, redshirting provides the right amount of education and experience *before* your new player actually takes on the full responsibility of their new position. You can accomplish this objective in a variety of ways. Some companies send their new hires away to a "boot camp" for a couple of weeks, where employees are immersed in the industry and learn important details about the company and their new job before they start. It's sort of a crash course in industry knowledge. If you choose this option, just be sure your company's boot camp is high value and high impact – your future superstars are too important to be sent off to a drab, bureaucratic onboarding program.

The best way to redshirt your new hires is to create an apprentice program at your company. Match your new players up with an established, trusted veteran, and let the new hire shadow the experienced player for three to five solid weeks. Some companies even let new hires act as the veteran's personal assistant, reading executive correspondence and sitting in on strategic meetings in order to better understand the inner workings of the business.

An apprentice program works for a simple reason: humans learn by immersion and osmosis. If you've hired the right person, your new player is a passionate, excited individual who is eager to learn from your business' best performers, so it's important to provide your future superstar with the right mentorship. In college football, they matched me up with the starting left guard so that I could learn the position perfectly. I studied every move he made, looked at every game situation on film, and thoroughly examined how he handled everything the opposing defense threw at him. A&M's apprentice program worked wonders for me on the gridiron, and it will set your rookies up for rapid success in your business, too – I guarantee it!

"There is no question in my mind that when a player is devoted to making himself the best he can be on all levels, that this is the greatest contribution he can make to his team"
~ Chris Valletta

Let's recap: In order to build a championship business team, you must properly prepare your players for game day. Establish a redshirt program that's carefully designed to develop the skills and experience necessary to be effective in your company and industry. Tell your future superstars that you know they are terrific at what they do, but they need to get accustomed to the "speed" of your industry, and they need to become familiar with the winning system you've designed before you can unleash them on your corner of the business world. Match them up with the superstar veterans at your company, and give them time to watch and learn. In just a few weeks, they'll be ready to tear into your industry.

"Always pick and surround yourself with teammates that are better than you. This will force you to elevate your game, drive your business, and ultimately ride their shoulders to success."
~ Warren Barhorst, CEO Iscential

Team WORKS! – Chapter 6

Meetings and Preparation

Marathon meetings are team killers. Show your players that perfect meetings bring perfect preparation.

"There are no secrets to success. It is the result of preparation, hard work, and learning from failure."
~ *Colin Powell*

Preparation means success, period. You've probably heard it so often that the idea has become a bit hackneyed, and hearing the concept in any of its various incarnations may make you involuntarily roll your eyes. But that doesn't mean it's not a critical aspect of building a championship business team, so it's sometimes helpful to view preparation from the opposite angle: if you don't prepare enough and in the right way, you will either get lucky enough to just barely squeak by, or, more likely, you'll fail miserably.

I like to think of preparation in two distinct contexts: short-term and long-term. Both are critically important to achieving business and athletic success, and both of them require the same keen attention to detail – JB Grimes' Little Things again – in order to provide the results you're seeking.

Long-term preparation focuses on developing and improving your team's baseline capability and capacity. This aspect is akin to an athlete's lifelong commitment to outstanding physical fitness. The athletes you watch on television don't just embark on a physical fitness "crash course" a couple of weeks prior to the start of the season. Biomechanics, metabolism, and neural wiring just don't work that way. Instead, world-class athletes train several hours a day, four to six days per week, for years on end in order to develop the strength, skill, agility, balance, endurance, and speed necessary to achieve success in their sport.

In the business world, long-term preparation involves developing a deep background of knowledge and expertise in your industry or specialty. Champions in the real estate business know their market inside and out, and are familiar with all of the major transactions going on at any given time in their territory. They form an innate sense of the direction their market seems to be trending long before the pundits catch on. Software business champions stay abreast of new capabilities as they develop, and clearly understand the nuanced differences between various competitors' offerings. Successful marketing pros have extensive experience in many different advertising and marketing media, and fluently speak the arcane language of marketing data and metrics. Regardless of your sport or business, long-term preparation provides the backdrop and expertise for the specific, short-term preparation you'll need in order to succeed in your everyday business engagements.

"For me, winning isn't something that happens suddenly on the field when the whistle blows and the crowds roar. Winning is something that builds physically and mentally every day that you train and every night that you dream."
~ Emmitt Smith, Dallas Cowboys Running Back

I view short-term preparation as those things you need to accomplish in order to be successful in a specific business setting. Effective short-term preparation requires a specific and well-defined objective. In football, our goal was always to defeat the next team on our schedule, and our short-term preparation involved practicing just those plays from our massive playbook that we anticipated using against the particular defense we were facing next. We studied films of our upcoming opponents' recent games in order to learn all we could about their personnel, strategies, strengths, and weaknesses (we'll spend more time on this extremely important concept in the next chapter). If they had a particularly strong player at a given defensive position, we practiced "double-teaming" techniques to neutralize him by ganging up on him. We studied the defense's alignment and formations in order to determine whether they held any clues about which tricks the defense might have up their sleeves on any given play. Our short-term preparation was designed to give us the best chance of making the most out of our strengths – built up over the years of our long-term preparation effort - while taking maximum advantage of our opponents' weaknesses.

Our long-term preparation gave us the basic football skills necessary to be successful, and our short-term work focused all of that basic football skill in the direction that gave us the best chance of winning the next game on our schedule. Championship businesses need exactly the same combination of efforts in order to dominate their corner of the market. Each player's individual expertise, developed over time, equips him or her with the foundational business skills they'll bring to bear in each situation; your team's short-term preparation will teach each player how to best use their hard-earned talents to win the upcoming sales bid, knock the technology demonstration out of the park, dazzle the board of directors, or roll out your new product on time and under budget.

As the player-coach of your championship business team, it's your responsibility to set the pace and the strategy for your team's long- and short-term preparation efforts. While we won't spend any time discussing how to develop a preparation strategy specific to your niche, I'll just say that there's good news: your team prep strategy is a natural extension of your overarching business strategy, and follows directly from the way you've positioned your company to compete in your market. If you're doing your own homework in your industry, you won't have any trouble identifying the specific skills your people need to master.

"When you're prepared, you're more confident. When you have a strategy, you're more comfortable."
~ *Fred Couples*

In their own words: Super Bowl Champion Offensive Lineman Roman Oben

Information. Transformation. Application. How preparation helps us process information, evolve our knowledge, and win on game day.

As children, we're constantly given information and instruction. Once our experiences qualify us to take information, transform it, and apply it, then the habit-forming process takes place. This process can take time to solidify.

However, in the life of a football player, this three-step process has to happen almost immediately. Malcolm Gladwell, in the book, "Blink," discusses "split-second, spontaneous decision-making" as it applies to the game of basketball. The same concept holds true in football.

For example, during my days as a Tampa Bay Buccaneer, Jon Gruden's West Coast offensive system was known for being wordy and complex. There was great pressure to receive the information, transform it, and apply it in the few seconds it takes to hear the play, go to the line of scrimmage, digest the quarterback's audible, determine the alternate play as well as your responsibility and the responsibilities of your teammates, recognize the defense, and respond to any last-second defensive changes. It took a great deal of preparation to operate with complete competency when the play started. Any number of seemingly minor mistakes could result in a play not being successful.

In life and business, we often have little more than a few seconds to make decisions based on limited information. In my experience, those who are best at applying the tenets of "Information, Transformation, Application" are those who are best prepared. There is no substitute for putting in the hours to prepare yourself as thoroughly as possible.

My first post-NFL job was as an account executive selling

outdoor advertising, also known as billboard advertising space. One of my responsibilities was to conduct cold calls to local businesses to convince them that billboard advertising would increase their visibility to their target audiences, as opposed to more conventional advertising vehicles such as print, radio, and television.

I once made a cold call to a computer repair company. It was the last week of my employer's first quarter and it was crunch time – third and ten, and my team needed a touchdown for the win. We badly needed the business.

The call didn't start off well, as the business owner lamented that he didn't have any discretionary money for advertising. He complained about his company's gloomy financial situation, and said that he didn't believe in spending money on something if there wasn't a fully guaranteed return on investment.

It was 2010 and most businesses were still climbing out of the recession. I shared some historical information I had gleaned through my extensive research about companies that advertised during tough economic times. My data showed that those companies that invested in advertising despite the condition of the economy managed to grow by more than 200% in subsequent years, while companies who chose to cut back on the spending didn't grow much at all.

By taking the information about his computer repair store, transforming it to show that I was acutely aware of his business trends and current needs, and applying a concrete solution, I was able to win the difficult sale. The business owner signed up for a seasonal billboard that ran for two months. The advertising attracted and convinced customers to come in for annual virus checks and software updates, and helped generate a solid return on his investment.

I never would have won the sale if I hadn't thoroughly researched my market, remained calm and collected during a tough sales call, and relied on my solid preparation to produce a great result.

Where does the rubber meet the road regarding your business preparation strategy? In an unexpected place: your meetings.

Here's what I mean. Have you ever watched a football game in which the offensive team completely dominated the defense? These situations are a thing of beauty to behold: the offensive line controls the defense so handily that the quarterback seems to have eons to find an open receiver, and running backs seem to have wide-open spaces ahead of them to the goal line or first down marker. Receivers always seem to be one step ahead of the defenders, and have little problem finding lonely corners of the field unoccupied by opponents. In those circumstances, every move the offense makes seems to be carefully choreographed and rehearsed in advance, and the result is one thrilling play after another with the offense moving through the defense like a hot knife through butter.

If these situations seem to have a distinct sense of choreography about them, it's because they actually are thoroughly planned and rehearsed! Strange as it may sound at first, these feats of football efficiency and effectiveness only come into existence as a result of extremely efficient and effective meetings.

These aren't just any meetings. These are meetings on steroids - but I'm referring to their usefulness, not their duration! Coaches don't drone on about tangential, unhelpful subjects, and players never nap or daydream, because they might be called upon at any second to provide an answer to a very pointed question: "Valletta, what's your responsibility when the linebacker shades outside and the tackle angles play-side?" If that sounds like a hard question, it certainly would be if I were ever to be caught unprepared! But I wouldn't dare stumble in to a meeting like this without first having done my homework, as my ignorance would be immediately exposed. Worse, it would also demonstrate my lack of dedication to the team and our shared goals.

Hours of individual study precede such championship meetings, and players and coaches alike are thoroughly engaged.

Each individual contributes, collectively helping the team advance toward the ultimate goal: victory in the next game. You might say that in order for the team to fire on all cylinders on the field, it must first fire on all cylinders in the meeting room.

How do you achieve such a championship meeting? By now, you won't be at all surprised at my answer: by honoring the important Little Things!

"People who enjoy meetings should not be in charge of anything."
~ Thomas Sowell

First, you must treat each meeting as a strategic event. That means you need to have a very succinct, specific, and critically important answer to this question: "Why are we spending the time, effort and money to meet today?" Because you're allocating significant business resources to gather your team together, it's your job to ensure that the meeting's desired outcome warrants taking each team member away from their *real* jobs – winning new customers, satisfying existing clients, and improving your products and services – in order to spend time seated around the table with you. Be sure you're serving a purpose that's worthy of your team's time and talents.

The first meetings during each week of football practice had the goal of communicating the outline of the coaching staff's strategy for the week's game preparation. "Pie-in-the-sky strategy sounds nice," you might say, "but what's the practical benefit?" Simple. These weren't theoretical, academic exercises, but served the very practical purpose of informing each player of the specific focus areas we would be responsible for learning and mastering during the week of practice leading up to the game.

As game day drew nearer, our meeting objectives shifted from communicating expectations to determining our level of preparation for the upcoming game, which gave these later meetings an examination-like atmosphere. We were expected to have put in the personal study time necessary to know our responsibilities absolutely cold. We took these meetings very seriously, as we might be called upon to answer detailed questions at any moment. We were keenly aware that starting jobs are won and lost just as frequently in the meeting room as on the playing field, and we all knew very well that the team had placed a great deal of trust in us to understand our roles as perfectly as possible.

Your championship business team meetings must have a similar laser focus. If you're accustomed to waxing poetic about arcane aspects of your business, or if you find yourself talking to your team members in a meeting without really having a point, or if you find yourself muttering those kinds of business platitudes that managers everywhere mutter when they don't really know what's going on or don't know what needs to be done (it's OK to admit it!), now is the perfect time to change your ways.

Just like in every other aspect of business, the big picture is comprised of many small things, so I'm going to give you my time-tested list of what goes into a championship-caliber business meeting. I've distilled this list from the thousands of meetings (good, bad, and miserable) that I've been party to over the years.

As you read this list, I'd like you to keep something very important in mind: while most business meetings are just what people do when they want to feel like they're doing something work-related *without really working*, the kind of meetings I advocate will require real w-o-r-k. You'll find that in order to inculcate a championship culture in your business team, you're going to have to invest the sweat equity required to run disciplined, effective, productive, efficient meetings. Save the baloney sessions for after hours and social settings, and give your absolute best effort to conducting professional meetings. There's no other way to build a championship business team.

So let's dive in.

1. Set a crystal-clear meeting objective. If you can't state your meeting objective in a clear, concise sentence, you need to go back to the drawing board. The objective also needs to be specific and measurable. For example, "We'd like to examine all of the ideas for our new marketing plan," is a terrific way to waste thousands of dollars in employee wages by conducting a meaningless marathon meeting. A championship objective would instead read like this: "We will emerge from this 20-minute meeting with an approved marketing strategy to support our East Coast expansion."

    Brainstorming sessions are no exception to the rule of having a rock-solid meeting objective. You should never convene a meeting with the objective of "brainstorming a few ideas for the new product improvement program." Instead, a winning objective might be to produce twenty viable ideas during your brainstorming meeting.

2. Keep it short and engaging! Even super-humans like your championship team members have a limited attention span. In fact, "Type A" personalities often have gnat-sized attention spans until they happen upon an interesting subject (then, they become mosquitos!), so it's important to keep the meeting moving.

    Just as importantly, every minute spent in a meeting is another minute that real work doesn't get done. No matter what your specific meeting objective might be, you're ultimately meeting in order to organize and focus your team members' future efforts, and it's critical not to mistake a successful meeting with real productivity. Your aim is to focus your team's effort in a specific direction, then set them free to get results. Shoot for a twenty-minute meeting. If you absolutely can't get it done in that amount of time, you've probably scoped your objective too broadly.

"Whatever you do, when you see the first person yawn in your meeting... STOP the meeting."
~ *Chris Valletta*

3. Establish an airtight agenda. Leave absolutely nothing to chance – after all, you're spending a bunch of *your* money by paying your team members to sit there with you in a meeting, so you'd better be getting maximum bang for your buck! Plan the meeting flow down to the minute, and strictly enforce the meeting timeline. Send this agenda to everyone on the attendance list a week in advance of your meeting, and solicit inputs regarding both the agenda and the attendee list. Incorporate those inputs, finalize the meeting's timeline, publish the final schedule, and then stick to it!

Reinforce your commitment to this timeline by having a printed copy pre-positioned at each member's spot around the table at the start of the meeting. And reinforce your commitment to the meeting's objective by placing it at the top of the agenda: "Close $50,000 in new business this month," or "Convert three clients from ABC Company to our company this quarter," or "Beat the University of Nebraska!"

If you're a rambler, prone to philosophical digressions (we all have our moments), it's in your business' best interest to appoint a Clock Master or Flow Enforcer to ride herd on the meeting agenda, and to keep you from derailing your own meeting. Deputize the Clock Master with the authority to cut a presentation short in order to stick to the timeline, and be sure they understand that part of their duty is to keep *you* on track and on time as well.

Demonstrating this level of commitment to a disciplined schedule and a meaningful agenda, while it may seem a little bit draconian, has an exceptionally important result: it forces everyone involved in your meeting – yourself included - to become very good at *having a point* when they open their mouth to speak, and communicating that point clearly and succinctly. Effective, efficient meeting communication requires you and your people to establish efficient and effective thinking habits, which have the happy side effect of shedding a great deal more light on every issue you tackle in your business.

How about those "fuzzier" objectives, such as brainstorming? Isn't it a bad idea to put a time limit on an objective as open-ended as coming up with new and innovative ideas? Absolutely not! It's not only a good idea, but it's absolutely necessary. A deadline has a strange effect on your team: your players end up producing *more* ideas under a deadline, not fewer, and these ideas tend to be *more viable* than ones produced during marathon brainstorming sessions. Songwriters often use a technique called "rapid idea prototyping," or RIP, where they set a timer for a ridiculously small amount of time – say an hour – to write and record a complete song, from start to finish. You'd be surprised to learn how many popular songs were written as rapidly as possible during an exercise such as this (refined later, of course, but the essence of the song came into being during a rapid idea prototyping session). Rest assured that establishing a timeline to meet your meeting objective will produce far greater results, in far less time, than allowing a creativity session to meander.

4. Invite the right people! This sounds like a no-brainer, but you'd be surprised at how many times an expert on a particular topic on the agenda is inadvertently left out of the meeting invitation list. Questions that experts would be able to easily address can quickly devolve into speculation sessions among the lesser informed, so take the time to ensure that your meeting contains the right subject matter experts.

5. Start on time. Vince Lombardi, one of the greatest football coaches in history, was famous for starting his meetings obsessively early. New players were horrified to discover that when they showed up ten minutes before a scheduled meeting, they were already ten minutes late! I don't advocate this kind of schedule skullduggery, but I do recommend an absolute commitment to starting on time. Fighter pilots go so far as to begin their pre-mission briefing by counting down the seconds to the appointed hour, having previously set their watches to the US master nuclear clock. If a given pilot isn't present in the briefing room when the countdown reaches zero, the late pilot doesn't fly that day! That might be taking things a little bit too far, but it does serve to make the point that starting on time sets the tone for the rest of the meeting, and such discipline and attention to detail translates into everything else you do in your business.

6. Begin with the end in mind. Even though your meeting objective is printed in bold at the top of your agenda, spend a couple of minutes reinforcing what you aim to achieve during the meeting. This focuses your team's attention, and gives you the opportunity to have your team members begin taking personal responsibility for their share of the team's objective. If all of your players, veterans and redshirts alike, take personal accountability for meeting the team's goal, then your team has twice the chance of achieving it.

    There is a very practical reason that you should start the meeting by talking about your goals and objectives: you need to foster your team's belief that they can achieve the goals you've set for them. Believing that you can achieve the goal is the most important step. Belief is power, power is action, and action generates results, so spending a few brief minutes to set the stage for what follows is time well spent.

7. Appoint a dedicated "meeting scribe," responsible for taking

copious notes during the meeting, summarizing action items at the meeting's conclusion, and sending the written summary to all participants promptly after the meeting concludes. If information comes up during the meeting that would benefit non-attendees, it's important to include them on the minutes as well.

Why go to all this trouble? First, bright ideas die quickly unless they become someone's tasked responsibility, so the scribe helps enforce the discipline of accountability. Second, publishing meeting minutes serves as a permanent record of the decisions you made during each meeting, which can serve a number of important legal, organizational, strategic, and administrative purposes. Finally, publishing minutes provides an official version of the proceedings, which reduces the possibility for misinterpretation and removes the temptation for employees to adopt creative interpretations that don't necessarily serve your team's best interests.

8. Allow absolutely no personal electronics. Unless it's for the purpose of a presentation, an electronic gadget can only hinder meeting progress. The only things you and your employees should bring to meetings are the agenda, and a pad and pen to take notes. You're spending good money to gather your employees for a very specific purpose, and the last thing you want is for them to be checking their stock portfolio, reading the joke of the month, or, more likely, keeping up with the daily flood of business email. Legitimate business correspondence is a far greater distraction than personal interests, and it's important to remove the temptation for your go-getters to compulsively check and respond to their office email. You need your team to be fully engaged in order to achieve your meeting objective.

9. Never settle for an opinion in place of a fact. If it's worth knowing, it's worth knowing right, and there's no substitute for hard data. There's obviously a place for informed

opinions, and you should clearly signal those occasions when you're interested in hearing a team member's judgment by actually using the words, "In your opinion." Otherwise, when it sounds to you like someone might be offering an opinion when you're looking for a factual input, it's easy to politely but firmly refocus the discussion by asking to see supporting data.

10. Set clear deadlines for follow-up actions. Every meeting you conduct should produce action items for your team members (after all, you're only meeting in order to focus your team's future efforts), and it's important to establish clear expectations for when those action items are due.

"If your son does exactly what I tell him to do, I promise that he will become a successful football player, and he'll become an even more successful person."
~ R.C. Slocum, former Texas A&M Head Coach, speaking in John and Michaela Valletta's living room in 1996 while recruiting their son Chris

Those are my ten laws for meeting success, and I adhere to them religiously in order to get the most out of every minute my team spends together. But there are two important Little Things that I weave into every aspect of my meetings. These details describe the way I deal with the people on my team during our time together.

First, I highlight individual and team successes publicly. Napoleon remarked that "men will die for ribbons," which is another way of saying that it is a basic human need to be acknowledged in front of our peers for our effort, contribution, and achievement. Recognition is motivating, inspiring, and positive for everyone involved; the high achievers feel satisfaction that their efforts are noticed and appreciated, and everyone else on the team feels a healthy competitive motivation to elevate their game in order to win recognition next time.

You should set aside dedicated recognition time during your meeting agenda to hand out formal awards, but it's equally important to acknowledge a killer presentation or keen insight right on the spot. Immediate feedback is a terrific motivator, and serves to positively reinforce the level of quality that you value in your business. Other team members take notice, and begin to shoot for similar levels of quality in their work as well. In this way, you enforce standards without having to do any real enforcement, and your team strives to meet your high standards because they know you appreciate and acknowledge their efforts and results.

On the other side of the coin, if there's ever any need to correct or adjust an employee's efforts or focus, *never* do so publicly. Your employees generally know when they're caught underprepared or when they perform below expectations, and public chastisement serves no useful purpose. In fact, it changes the motivation source for your entire team. Instead of striving and achieving greatness because it's a competitive, fun, positive experience, your team members subconsciously begin trying not to fail. It's a far less productive team dynamic, and it usually has poor results. When football teams stop striving for excellence and instead start playing not to lose, they instantly start to over-think and underperform, and that's a deadly combination on the gridiron as well as in your business.

Sometimes you'll hear a presentation in one of your meetings, and you won't know immediately whether or not you agree with your employee's conclusions. In those situations, it's extremely important to suspend your judgment until you have a clearer understanding of the issue. Never undermine a player's efforts in front of everyone else in the meeting. Instead, enlist your team member's support to help you better understand their perspective. You can say something like this: "You've given me food for thought, and I'd like you to help me understand this a bit better. Let's get together to talk more about it after the meeting."

I use those two techniques – praising in public, and suspending any judgment until I can talk to my team members individually - to ensure accountability without undermining motivation. This helps my team stay unified, positive, inspired, and effective.

"Rest assured, your #1 competitor is working just as hard as you are... This is the moment when the champions separate themselves from the rest and go above and beyond what their competition could even think of."
~ Chris Valletta

Great, so we now know how to run a productive, efficient meeting. So what? As I pointed out earlier, while perfect meetings demand a great deal of work, meetings themselves aren't actually work! You're not winning clients or building more amazing products while you're sitting in a meeting. But if you follow the guidelines I've outlined above, your meetings will have the same effect that a fireman's nozzle has on the water: it focuses all of the resources and energy in the right direction to do the most good. Only instead of putting out fires, you'll be igniting the fire of productivity and excellence as you focus your team's long- and short-term preparations to achieve your business objectives.

I don't believe that practice makes perfect; instead, I believe that *perfect* practice leads to perfect execution in the game. Your meetings should guide your team to prepare perfectly, focusing the right amount of effort and energy on the right areas to help your team members become excellent at the Little Things that will secure victory.

But your role doesn't stop there. Once the meeting breaks, it's time to accomplish the *real* work, and it's your job to make sure that the execution matches your expectations. Your team will likely split into functional groups to further define and execute the tasks that lead to achieving your objectives, and it's important for you to remain engaged and involved as the preparation unfolds.

For example, early in his career, my brother John was a marketing executive for one of the major auto manufacturers, and one of his responsibilities was to pitch new campaign ideas to the executive team. These pitches were complex, and contained plans for many different marketing campaign elements such as television, print, radio, in-dealership, and online media. John and his team regularly crushed these presentations, and that's no accident – he used a deliberate, proven method.

John first held a group meeting (using the principles I've mentioned in this chapter) to lay out his objectives, and then his team split off into functional groups such as layout, design, photography, radio, print, TV, etc., to further discuss the task. After the smaller groups fleshed out concepts for the pitch, John brought the entire team back together, and asked the functional managers to discuss their concepts with him. Once he was satisfied the team had a winning approach, John tied the individual pieces together to execute the strategy, and he continued to monitor each team's progress as they developed their portion of the presentation.

After each department finished with their individual piece of the puzzle, John assembled each unit, evaluated their work, and gave his approval for inclusion in the final presentation. This is just like the coaching staff producing a winning strategy, but just like in football, a winning strategy isn't even half the battle. Now it's time for the players to practice their individual role until it becomes second nature. This portion of the preparation phase involves rehearsal after rehearsal, with adjustments occurring at every step of the way to maximize the impact and "wow factor" of their presentation. John made inputs throughout the process, and by the time his team stood in front of the executives, he had every confidence that they were as prepared as possible.

John's successful approach to his multi-million dollar marketing plan pitches was very similar to the way a football team prepares for a big game. When my 1998 college football team was facing Nebraska, the top team in the nation, we knew that we had our work cut out for us. Nebraska's players were big, fast, and extremely well-coached. We began our preparations a week early to ensure that we left no stone unturned in our search for any exploitable advantages we might have enjoyed over them. We scoured hours of film to uncover any weaknesses and discover how we best matched up against their enormously talented players. Our coaches ran well-organized meetings, and our players showed up to each meeting prepared to answer the toughest questions about their assignments on each kind of play in the upcoming game. We left our meetings and hit the practice field with a crystal clear understanding of the precise skills we'd need to perfect in order to beat the top-ranked team in the nation.

We set our minds on preparing for a victory, and that's exactly what happened. It was a tough slog, and Nebraska nearly rallied in the fourth quarter, but our perfect preparations resulted in an amazing upset victory.

In addition to getting your team into championship form, the preparation phase is useful for another extremely important reason: it is a key opportunity to further evaluate your new hires as they grow into their new roles in your business. As we discussed in Chapter 4, you're never really 100% sure what kind of a player you're getting when you hire a new team member, and while you may feel confident that you've chosen a terrific addition for your championship team, nothing beats time and experience to tell you whether or not your intuition was accurate. As the team works together toward a common goal of increasing sales, winning a big contract, or rolling out the next generation of groundbreaking product, pay close attention to the contributions your new additions make. Do they consistently demonstrate more of the qualities that made you hire them in the first place? Do they work smoothly and seamlessly with the rest of your team? If so, your recruiting and redshirting efforts paid off. If not, it might be time to start thinking about making a change.

Speaking of redshirting, preparation activities provide a terrific training opportunity for your redshirting program. Adding your new hires to the mix during the preparation phase gives them a great opportunity to see your team in action, become familiar with norms and standards, and learn the specifics of their future responsibilities.

"People who work together will win, whether it be against complex football defenses, or the problems of modern society."
~ *Vince Lombardi*

Preparing to meet your team's objective is 99% of the game. Set specific, measurable objectives to guide your team's efforts. Follow my ten meeting laws to conduct perfect meetings that set the tone and focus your team's energy in the right direction. Remain engaged with all the elements of your team as they develop their portion of your business strategy, and bring the entire team together to practice, practice, and practice some more. Rehearse, revamp, and repeat the process until flawless execution becomes second nature. At the end of the process, you and your team will be a well-oiled machine in championship condition.

Team WORKS! – Chapter 7

Watch Film

Championship teams in business don't make the same mistakes twice. Rest assured that your competition is studying your every move!

Icouldn't figure out what the heck was going on. My Texas A&M team had traveled to Lafayette, Louisiana to take on the Louisiana State Ragin' Cajuns, a relatively small school playing in the Sun Belt Conference, in front of their capacity crowd of 30,000 fans. With fifteen future-NFL players on our roster and a powerhouse reputation, my A&M team was a heavy favorite, and the game shouldn't have been close.

But things hadn't unfolded that way. The fired up Ragin' Cajuns had taken full advantage of the opportunity to play a major college program, and they were more than ready for us. We should have been well on our way to a 40+ point victory, but late in the game, we weren't on the winning end of the score, and we were rapidly running out of time.

The Louisiana State defensive line seemed to stay excep-tionally disciplined during our running plays, filling each of the gaps between our offensive linemen and preventing our running backs from gaining any appreciable ground. During our passing plays, they seemed to be the precise opposite, pinning their ears back and rushing our quarterback with abandon. It seemed like the defense predicted our every move before we made it.

In fact, that's exactly what they did. Were they clairvoyant? Omniscient? Lucky? None of the above, but they didn't need to be. They were just better prepared. They had studied films of our previous games extremely thoroughly, and learned that our offensive line stances varied ever so slightly from play to play depending on whether the upcoming play was a run or a pass. On running plays, our offensive linemen had more of their weight resting on their hands (offensive linemen place one hand on the ground in what's called a "three-point stance"); this allowed us to fire forward very quickly when the play began in order to block the defensive linemen out of the way of our running back. On passing plays, their coaches noticed that we leaned a little bit further back in our stances, which allowed us to fall back into our pass protection more quickly.

The Louisiana coaching staff instructed their defensive players to look very closely at our stances prior to the start of each play, and it didn't take long for them to catch on to this important giveaway. When I had my weight in the back of my stance, the defensive lineman across from me would send a signal to the linebackers, and the linebackers would send a signal to the secondary (cornerbacks and safeties) letting them know that we were getting ready to run a pass play. Given that our offense chose an equal mix of running and passing plays, the giveaway of our uneven weight distribution in our stances allowed the defense to eliminate half of the possible plays that we could have run.

Our quarterback also dropped his left foot further back than his right on those plays when he had to move to his left. This fact wasn't lost on the well-prepared defense, and they were able to quickly shift their alignment to favor our left side, getting the jump on us.

These giveaways, or "tells," gave them a distinct advantage. They knew what was coming, which took away the element of surprise and allowed them to easily stymie our efforts. These subtle details weren't the only difference in the outcome of the game that day (I'm sad to report that the clock ran out while they had more points), but it certainly went a long way toward keeping our potent offense bottled up.

This was one of the biggest victories in Louisiana State's history – so much so that as the clock wound down to zero, the fans rushed the field and tore down the goalposts. A picture of the scoreboard ended up on the front page of the local newspapers, and the same picture adorned their football program's media guide for the following season.

We were out-prepared - and consequently, outplayed – by a team with less size, strength, and talent. However, their incredibly focused preparation made up for their physical short-falls, and they performed masterfully as a result. The experience taught me a powerful lesson about the importance of studying game and practice films as part of the preparation process. We used to have a saying in football about watching film: "The big eye in the sky never lies." We may not have thought we were giving away our intentions before each play, but if we had studied our own stances prior to the start of various types of offensive plays as closely as our Louisiana State competitors had, it's entirely possible that we would have caught and eliminated this dead giveaway, taking away their advantage.

How important is film study? Teams invest many thousands of dollars in video cameras to cover each position on the field on every play. They hire analysts whose only job is to study opposing teams' films and produce a highly detailed catalog of tendencies, formations, plays, and personnel packages in various types of game situations. Football teams take Sun Tzu's advice to heart: *"So it is said that if you know your enemies and know yourself, you can win a hundred battles without a single loss. If you only know yourself, but not your opponent, you may win or may lose. If you know neither yourself nor your enemy, you will always endanger yourself."* In our case on that disappointing day in Lafayette, our enemy knew us better than we knew ourselves!

While it's rare for businesses to have such a sterling opportunity to gain intelligence on their competitors (nobody films and broadcasts their board meetings, for example), studying your competition is an extremely important part of becoming a championship business team. In fact, having a good idea of your competitor's next major move may mean the difference between success and failure.

Take the ongoing battle between US automotive giants Ford and General Motors. The companies have been locked in close competition for over a century (some analysts call it "the other hundred-year war"), each vying to pry market share from the other. Both companies invest huge sums of money to discover what the other might be up to, as learning of a new car line or sales promotion in advance of your opponent's rollout allows you to prepare an appropriate counterpunch. Likewise, both companies take great pains to keep their future plans a secret.

In one instance, GM's secret-keeping apparatus bested Ford's intelligence-gathering team, and the Ford camp didn't catch wind of the GM Employee Discount Program until GM rolled out the revolutionary promotion. GM's EDP allowed general consumers to receive as large a discount as the auto maker's own employees are eligible to receive, and it's safe to say that the public jumped at the chance. In fact, EDP was the most successful promotion in automotive history, and GM sold over 50,000 cars in a two-month period.

The Ford team was completely unprepared for the attack. On its heels, Ford didn't come out with the "Ford Family Plan" until months later, after GM's sales had long since left them in the dust.

How do you avoid having a Ford experience? Invest heavily to thoroughly understand your competitors' positioning, product nuances, and developmental pipeline. As you're assembling your championship team, don't neglect the market intelligence and analysis role. Find a sharp, talented, data-driven analyst to head your intelligence department, and provide them with the necessary resources to produce cogent, relevant, and timely information. If you're not yet in a position to invest this heavily to monitor your competition, charge each of your other functional areas to routinely evaluate their counterparts in your industry. You won't always be able to successfully predict your competitors' next move, but a thriving analysis function is the price of admission in a competitive business environment. You'll have no prayer of competing without it.

"Champions keep playing until they get it right."
~ Billie Jean King

As I mentioned earlier, watching films isn't just about discovering your competitors' tendencies and "tells." It's also about sharpening your own team's skills. In fact, "scouting" your own team is one of the most important techniques you can use to develop a winning business team.

It's not just a football thing. Fighter pilots record their displays during every mission, and then painstakingly reconstruct what happened during the flight as they debrief the sortie. They spend hours reviewing how each pilot used the systems on the airplane, and how they digested and responded to the audio and visual cues available to help them make sense of a complicated situation. The process lasts many times longer than the flight itself – it's not uncommon for the post-flight film study session for a two-hour sortie to last ten hours! This isn't for fun or entertainment, but to ultimately prepare them to make better decisions, faster, and to execute those decisions more precisely the next time they fly. A ten-hour film study session is probably a bit extreme, but we can certainly take a lesson from the football and flying communities to help us model our approach to business preparations.

Here's how you might approach a self-assessment effort. If you have an important presentation coming up, set up a video camera to record your team's practice sessions. After each session, go through the video with them. You'll have two objectives: first, make sure you highlight all of the positive things you notice about the practice presentation. Your primary purpose is to recognize and reinforce great work. If one of your team members exhibits tremendous poise, be sure to compliment her and use her as an example. Single out the players that made a great comment or a perfect point during the presentation. If the transitions between topics are seamless, be sure to compliment the team on their terrific preparation in this area.

This is something my college football coach did very well. For instance, if I just flattened a linebacker into the Texas dirt, the coach would always shout out, "Great job Valletta! That was perfectly executed!" He could have just told me that I did a good job, but the coach always made it a point to make a big deal out of the positives – he knew it was tremendously motivating.

"If you are going to be a champion, you must be willing to pay a greater price"
~ *Bud Wilkenson*

Your second objective as you review the filmed performance of your team's practice sessions is to find and fix any problem areas. For example, if you notice distracting hand movements, or a mismatch between the narrative and the visual aids, or a point that isn't made compellingly, it's important to arrive at a specific solution before moving on.

This is an art form in itself, and you should begin by asking your team members' impressions of the problem area. Quite often, they'll already have identified the issue and have an idea of how to fix it. Letting them take the lead to talk about how to improve the presentation gives them confidence that you value their input, and gives them greater buy-in to the eventual solution. Of course, you'll guide and facilitate the discussion, but encouraging a collaborative and collegial process will reap far greater rewards and generate dramatically better future performance than merely providing your opinion on every issue that comes up.

There's an extremely important concept to keep in mind as you review and critique your team's performance: hold yourself to an even higher standard than you expect of your team, and publicly critique your own performance. I cannot overstress how important it is for you to be transparent about your own short-comings. You will lose the respect of your team, and you will eventually lose your ability to lead them at all, if they sense any hypocrisy whatsoever from you. The world's best leaders are humble, credible, and approachable, and providing an honest and no-holds-barred critique of your own performance is essential to retaining your team members' respect and loyalty.

The same principles apply as you study less straightforward business efforts. For example, if a new advertising initiative doesn't achieve the projected response rate, it's important to spend the necessary time to discover the root cause of the issue. This may take a significant level of effort, and may require you to ask a number of clarifying questions on your way to discovering what went wrong, but championship business teams don't quit until they've discovered the keys to improving their performance.

As you play detective, be very deliberate about highlighting the positive elements that you uncover en route to the smoking gun. It is easy to focus on negative aspects during your review of the things that led up to a disappointing set of results, but it's in precisely these circumstances that you should devote *more* attention to well-executed elements. Your people can't help but feel some discouragement over sub-par results, so highlighting the positive things you discover as you search for the root cause will help keep your players motivated and confident.

All aspects of your business can benefit from a thorough "film review," which will afford you many opportunities to reinforce positive, effective performances while you adjust the less-successful aspects of your business. Schedule these reviews at regular intervals, and be sure to publicly praise your top performers.

"One heartbeat, one voice, one team. When all three are together, you've got a championship trophy in clear sight."
~ *Chris Valletta*

Your film reviews will serve a third purpose as well: the self-assessment process will train your team members to develop a keen eye for the important Little Things themselves, and it won't be long before they notice things that even escape you. In essence, you'll be teaching your players to become player-coaches, and you'll notice that the improvement in their performance begins to accelerate as they grow into this expanded role.

The film review process even works when you don't have the opportunity to film your team in action, but it requires more effort and professionalism on your part. First, you need to take copious notes during the performance (which may be a presentation, a sales call, an important meeting with a client, etc.), highlighting your impressions as the event unfolds. Later, as you review your notes with your team, apply the same priorities: reinforce the positive, and collaborate with your players to improve the less-than-stellar moments. The major difference is that in the absence of film, you will only have your impressions as the "evidence" of an area that needs improving, so you'll need to be diplomatic about how you describe what you saw.

You can avoid contentious and counterproductive moments by using a little humility. Something along these lines works nicely: "I may not have heard you correctly, but I was confused during your cost discussion – would you mind walking me through that portion of your presentation again?" That way you'll involve your team members in the discovery process, and you won't unnecessarily place your players on the defensive.

"Study and remember every move you made, because after a while, you'll instinctively take the same steps that brought you to success in the past."
~ *Chris Valletta*

If you're not used to doing business this way, all of this evaluation and discussion may strike you as a bit unusual, but it's for a very good reason: championship teams leave no stone unturned in their quest to absolutely minimize the number of mistakes they make.

It's not possible to completely eliminate mistakes, but you should develop a healthy abhorrence of *repeated* mistakes. Einstein once defined insanity as doing the same thing over and over again, yet expecting a different result each time. Don't be an insane entrepreneur – take every necessary step to keep your team from being plagued by repeated errors. Repeat mistakes are game killers, and can even be team killers if left unchecked.

The best way to sweep errors out of your business is to view mistakes and miscues as terrific teaching tools, and spend the necessary time to get to the bottom of them. Find positive aspects to reinforce, and let your team members participate in finding a fix. Become religious about your "film review" process, and remain dedicated to the tough work of self-assessment and continuous improvement. It's the only way to create a championship team. Invest the time and effort necessary to learn as much as you can about your competitors, and you and your championship team will be on your way to market domination.

PART 3

THE EXECUTION

Team WORKS! – Chapter 8

Game Day

Time to execute – Game Day means you leave nothing on the table

You've spent the time and energy to become excellent at the Little Things, and you've developed a champion's mental toughness by mastering your mindset. You've assembled your assistant coaches – your execs and department heads – and charged them with securing their domain and scouting the right players. You've spent countless hours assembling and growing a championship team. You've redshirted your young players, and they have grown quickly in your organization to learn your business and industry inside and out. You've conducted impeccably professional meetings and ensured your team's effort remains focused on attaining your business goals. You've run a bulletproof preparation process, and you've spent the necessary hours watching film to scout your competition and improve your own team's performance.

It's time to talk about game day.

Maybe you have a big event fast approaching that will set the course for your business, such as an important sales pitch, a new product launch, or a key vendor selection. Or, more likely, you might have a succession of big events on the immediate horizon, with each one having potentially game-changing impact. That's life as usual in the business world, which is not unlike a football game: it's comprised of a series of smaller events, called plays, which in aggregate determine the game's outcome. The same holds true for the success or failure of your entire business; excellent performance during every play – every client pitch, marketing campaign, and product delivery opportunity – will determine whether you attain your championship goals.

Sound a little like the Little Things? Absolutely. But now it's time to execute under the bright lights and added pressure of a game day environment. As the player-coach, it's your job to guide your team through the process. You'll need to help them stay in control of their emotions, keep focused on what's important, stay confident in their preparation and ability, and handle any curveballs with skill, style and grace.

Are you ready? Is today the day that you raise the metaphorical championship trophy? If you've followed the athlete's playbook for building a championship business team, I guarantee that you are better prepared than the vast majority of your competitors. Your preparation has been focused and extensive, and it's time for your team to shine. Game day is when you reap the rewards for all of the hard work and dedication. Game day should be fun, exciting, exhilarating, and, ultimately *profitable* for your business.

> *"It doesn't matter who can score points, it's who can get the ball to the scorer."*
> *~ Larry Bird*

As an athlete, I used to love game days. I would wake up with a big smile on my face, and I knew deep in my heart I had prepared as well as I possibly could. I had followed the training and study program that my coaches had laid out for me to the letter, cutting no corners. I felt confident that I had done everything I could possibly do to be the best-prepared offensive lineman on the field.

I had a sense of quiet confidence that seemed to be gleaming from my body, and my teammates felt the same way. We knew, especially before the 1998 Nebraska game, that we had prepared harder and longer, but most importantly, *better* than our opponent had. We knew that we were extremely well-coached. We each felt ready to perform with skill, mental toughness, and physical endurance, and that's exactly what we did.

Now it's your turn to get your team geared up to perform to their fullest potential on game day. Whether it's a key presentation, a product or service rollout, or a head-to-head show down with your competition, it's up to you to get your team ready to play at the moment it matters most. How do successful player-coaches accomplish this? The time-honored pregame speech, of course!

"My thoughts before a big race are usually pretty simple. I tell myself: Get out of the blocks, run your race, stay relaxed. If you run your race, you'll win."
~ Carl Lewis

As with all things in business and athletics, putting together an effective pregame speech is an art form. As my humorous run-in with Warren Sapp on my first day as a Tampa Bay Buccaneer illustrates, getting your team mentally ready to play isn't always about getting your players whipped into an emotional frenzy. In fact, your challenge will more likely be to *reduce* your players' emotion and nervous energy to help ensure they perform at their best. World-class athletes know that poor performance is far more likely when they're uptight, and your world-class business team members are no different. They'll be most effective when they're relaxed and confident. The great coaches know this as well, and they are skilled at helping their team reduce the emotion level and nervous tension before the start of a big game. Most people associate Hall of Fame coach Vince Lombardi, one of the all-time greats, with unmatched intensity and discipline. Those were certainly two of his greatest attributes, but Lombardi was equally skilled at helping his players relax before kickoff. In December of 1966, when Lombardi's Green Bay Packers faced off against the arch-rival Dallas Cowboys in the NFL championship game, Lombardi's entire pregame speech consisted of a single joke! The laugh broke the tension, and helped his team settle in for the hard-fought slog that lay ahead. Green Bay won a very close game, and went on to defeat Kansas City in the first Super Bowl in history.

Not only is there no value in getting too hyped up before a big event, but excessive emotion can also be a hazard. Erik Williams, who enjoyed a long career as a Dallas Cowboy and became one of the best offensive tackles in the NFL, provides a good object lesson. Before one game, Erik got himself so amped up that when his name was called during team introductions, he ran out on the field so fast that he pulled his hamstring! He missed the entire game, and three more after that, due to his misplaced pregame exuberance.

While your business team isn't likely to suffer any physical injuries due to a lack of mental discipline, your team members' nerves, anxiety, and over-motivation is a serious risk to championship performance. If you've followed the playbook to this point, your team is extremely well prepared for the big event, and your players all have the skills and expertise to perform brilliantly. Your only job before the big event is to reinforce your players' rock solid belief that the team is 100% unstoppable.

How do you know what your team needs in the way of a pregame speech? There's no substitute for experience where leadership is concerned, but I'll give you the game day guidelines that I follow when I prepare my championship business teams for a big event. I like to gather everyone on my team into a private, quiet room. I keep the atmosphere light but quiet, and I let my team sit quietly for several minutes. My players use this time to reflect on their preparation and review important facts or strategies before a key presentation, sales pitch, or client meeting.

As a football player, I used to love the quiet time before a game. I'll always remember RC Slocum, my college coach, standing silently at the front of the room with all of his assistant coaches next to him. Everyone in the locker room remained quiet, but we all felt the rumble of 85,000 ecstatic fans above us. It was an amazing and unforgettable environment, but it often required every bit of our mental toughness to remain relaxed and confident and avoid having our excitement turn to nervousness and anxiety. On the best days, as we reflected on our preparation efforts and the nuances of our game plan, we felt perfectly confident. Before some games, we felt a sense of inevitable victory, and that perfectly relaxed but eager mindset usually brought magic moments on the field. I foster a similar environment (minus the roaring crowd, of course) in my pregame meeting with my business team, and my players take advantage of the few minutes of quiet time I set aside for mental preparation.

"The best teams in the world are filled with players who know how to motivate themselves. When a coach delivers an effective pregame speech, it puts those players in a mental state that no one can touch."
~ Chris Valletta

After I've allowed my team to reflect quietly for a few minutes, I ask one of my seasoned veterans to share a few words with the team. My veterans have been on my team for countless big events, and I have complete confidence in their leadership and judgment – because I have trained them, watched them grow, and helped them learn to become effective leaders with a fantastic sense of the moment. Occasionally, they'll very briefly remind the team of an important key to success for the upcoming task, or go over a significant detail or two. My vets know that the pregame environment is no place for minutiae, and they only offer valuable inputs that help keep the team focused.

Once any last-minute technical or tactical details are out of the way, my veterans take a moment to reinforce their faith in the team's preparation, skill, and expertise. They thank their colleagues and charges for the terrific effort they've contributed to getting the team ready for the big event, and they express their pride in the team's accomplishments. Above all, my veterans know to keep their comments genuine, heartfelt, and **brief**. Ten or twenty seconds is plenty of time to convey the right meaning.

I thank my veterans for their effort and leadership, and then it's my turn to address my championship business team before we "take the field." This is absolutely no time for business-school platitudes or hackneyed motivational bromides (there's never any place for that crap, but you should take extra care to avoid it on game day!). Everything that comes out of my mouth comes straight from my gut. I look my team members in the eye as I address them, and I thank them for their hard work and excellent preparation. I congratulate them for what they have achieved and, more importantly, what they have *become* as they've prepared for this day.

I spend absolutely no time talking about details or analyzing what might lie ahead – the time for analysis and deconstruction is long past, and I don't insult my team's thorough preparation by revisiting any of those topics. I just let them know that I have complete confidence in their ability and preparation.

That's all I say, and that's all that you should tell your team before your big event. They don't need you to motivate them, because you have recruited, hired, trained, and fielded a team full of self-motivated superstars. They don't need you to remind them of any important details, because you have built a team full of experts with a passionate commitment to doing the Little Things right. Don't try to unveil some magical formula for victory just minutes before kickoff, because if you're following the championship team-building playbook, everything you've done in your business, and every task you've placed before your team, has been aimed at preparing them perfectly for the big moment.

There is literally nothing left for you to say, so don't fill the silence. Express your gratitude, pride, and confidence in your team, and then lead them out to the big event. Your pregame speech shouldn't last more than a minute or two.

"Any Questions? Comments? Observations?
All right boys, let's go."
~ Coach Mike Clark, Texas A&M; pre-game speech against
Nebraska 1998

A former boss of mine illustrated this concept perfectly. I sold radio advertising throughout Texas, and we had worked extremely hard to secure a thirty-minute appointment with a large company's marketing director. We had done an enormous amount of research to discover the company's advertising goals, and had assembled an airtight advertising plan to help them meet their objectives. I had rehearsed my pitch dozens of times, and I knew all of the facts, figures, rules, regulations, and contingencies for our entire campaign forward and backward. Our team had put in the necessary work to craft a terrific plan, and I was well prepared for the sales presentation. There was a great deal at stake – it was an extremely important deal for my company, and my commission on this single sale would make for a nice **annual** income. No pressure.

My company president knew how much was at stake, and he also knew how hard my team and I had worked to put our best foot forward. During my three-hour car trip to the client's headquarters on the day of my presentation, he phoned me to deliver his pregame speech. He said, "Chris, you've worked hard, you're completely ready, and I've seen your presentation a dozen times in our preparation meetings. I know that you have put together the best radio advertising program that they will ever see. Go get 'em!" It was the perfect pregame speech, and I walked into the client's office relaxed, confident, and ready to perform at my best.

"When it comes time to execute, just let your helmet do the talking. Your performance will speak volumes."
~ Chris Valletta

Regardless of the coach's oratory skills, no pregame speech ever put points on the scoreboard, and game day is all about execution. If done well, your pregame talk has helped to put your team in the right frame of mind to achieve fantastic results, but it's now time to *get it done.*

There's no magic pill for perfect execution, but there is an extremely important concept to incorporate into your team's approach to game day: There is an enormous difference between a well-*rehearsed* performance and a well-*prepared* performance. Well-rehearsed events consist of memorized lines and prearranged demonstrations. These performances are a dime a dozen, and don't make the championship cut because the preparation is usually only superficial. Any changes, curveballs, unexpected questions, or random instances of bad luck can rapidly scuttle even the best-*rehearsed* – but poorly *prepared* - performance. A single question from the audience can cause a presentation to fail completely if the presenter doesn't fully understand their material and have the mental and emotional wherewithal to arrive at an effective answer under the pressure of the moment. I've seen many presentations derailed by an innocuous question simply because the presenters tried to regurgitate memorized lines and weren't prepared to simply communicate concepts they had actually mastered.

On the other hand, world-class teams demonstrate their perfect preparation by handling unexpected circumstances with skill and confidence. True preparation certainly involves a great deal of rehearsal, and your team should always put on a terrific show, but a properly prepared team will have mastered the concepts so thoroughly that they can handle curveballs with poise and proficiency. In order to execute at the championship level, your team members must be able to pull apart the entire program, product, or pitch, and reassemble it *on the fly* in a way that incorporates the new information or solves the unexpected problem.

This requires your team members to emerge from your training program with two critical attributes. First, as we've seen in previous chapters, your players must have thoroughly mastered all of the Little Things in their domain in order to be successful on game day. Second, championship execution also requires your team members to remain calm, cool, and collected under pressure. Anxiety causes mental gridlock, so your players need to develop immunity to anxiety under pressure.

"From the gridiron to the boardroom; with a helmet or a briefcase...the battles can be just as nasty. The key is to be nastier than the other guy."
~ Chris Valletta, as heard on The Apprentice, Season 4 with Donald Trump

As I mentioned in Chapter 3, the most successful players are the ones who most successfully ignore pressure, because they know that cool confidence creates the right mental environment to perform at their best when unexpected events pop up. So while it's important that your team begins the game with the right mindset, it is absolutely critical that your players have the mental discipline to *stay* relaxed, confident, and focused when surprises appear.

"That's great, but how?" you might be asking. The answer won't surprise you: I teach my team members the same self-mastery techniques that I outlined in Chapter 3. As we saw, anxiety is always about the future or the past, and is never about the present moment. When the CEO of a prospective client company asks a stumper of a question that puts your sales team on the spot, any anxiety your players experience is caused not by the question itself, but by your players' worry that their answer will not be good enough. If you think about it carefully, you'll realize that the anxiety is actually caused by worrying about a *future* issue, and has nothing to do with the issue *right now*. The issue *right now* – the very next moment after the question leaves the CEO's mouth - is much simpler: your players just need to calmly call on their extensive expert knowledge and under-standing of the subject matter to produce the best answer available. Nothing more than that should occupy their thoughts, even for a second.

There's no anxiety in this process at all. Because the conscious mind can only entertain one thought at a time, any worry about the future actually *prevents* people from producing an effective solution right now, when it matters most. Your championship team will perform at their peak in pressure situations if you can help them become adept at ignoring everything that isn't related to *the present moment*. The task at hand is never to worry about the future, even if the future situation is only a few minutes away. Instead, championship teams know that the task at hand is always to use their expertise to find a great solution. This is the essence of poise, and it is absolutely essential for success in a dynamic environment.

"Character cannot be developed in ease and quiet. Only through experiences of trial and suffering can the soul be strengthened, vision cleared, ambition inspired and success achieved."
~ Helen Keller

Unexpected events challenge champions' poise all the time on the gridiron. During the game against Nebraska in 1998, the Cornhusker offense threw a completely new formation at our defense. It wasn't a formation that Nebraska had ever used before, and we had no scouting film that showed them using this new scheme. The sudden change was designed to cause confusion in the hope that one of our players would misread his responsibility, leaving an exploitable gap in our defense. But our coaching staff had prepared our team extremely well, and our players all thoroughly understood the fundamentals of football formations. We were able to make a single small adjustment and easily handle the new Cornhusker scheme. If our players had just memorized their responsibilities in specific situations without fully understanding the underlying concepts, they would have been lost.

"Those who dare to fail miserably can achieve greatly."
~ John F. Kennedy

The teams that just memorize solutions will inevitably fail when a new problem crops up that wasn't already engrained in their memory. But just like championship sports teams handle unexpected situations with calm skill, world-class business teams are always ready to handle contingencies, because the business world is full of unexpected game day events.

For example, I experienced a significant challenge during my radio advertising sales presentation to the marketing director of a large company. The sales meeting was moving along flawlessly until, half way through my presentation and 55-minutes into my 30-minute appointment, the head of marketing threw a curveball at me. Internally, the client company faced legal and policy restrictions that prevented them from implementing the advertising plan that my team and I had originally designed. This could have been a major setback – maybe even a deal-breaker – except that I was well prepared and not just well-rehearsed, and I remained calm and confident. I thoroughly understood every element of the campaign, so I was able to quickly devise and present an alternative approach.

How did my on-the-fly solution work? Not only did the marketing director sign the deal, but he also took me around his office to meet his staff! It was a terrific moment for my team, and it was only possible because I remained poised when the inevitable curveball appeared. Because I was thoroughly prepared and stayed cool under pressure, I was ready to knock it out of the park.

Game day doesn't just test the degree of preparation and skill of your individual players. Real-world events test whether your team's players work together effectively to get the job done. All athletic teams, and even the smallest business teams, have some degree of specialization among players. Offensive linemen generally can't throw passes, kick field goals, or cover an opponent's wide receivers as well as other players do. And no 185-lb wide receiver alive could stop a 330-lb defensive tackle from crushing the quarterback. It's equally true that you'd probably never send your world-class IT tech on a sales call, and you'd probably never send your best salesman to fix the office computer server. You've built a team comprised of players with functional specialties, but that's not the only type of team specialization that you can use to your advantage.

In addition to the formal specialization of expertise, there's also an informal distribution of talents within your team. For example, your operations lead may also have terrific public speaking skills, and your marketing guru may also have deep software expertise. As your team grows and gels together during the course of your training program, your players will begin to develop an innate sense of their teammates' unique skills and talents – even the "out-of-lane" abilities. Their confidence in each other will increase, and they'll come to rely on each other for much more than just those things that might fall within a formal organizational bucket.

This familiarity and confidence is an invaluable asset on game day. Championship business teams are adept at quickly finding the internal resources best positioned and prepared to conquer a pop-up challenge. Team members know each other so well that they effortlessly pass elements of a complex task between best-qualified members to create the best possible product.

This communication and teamwork must not be limited only to the formal functions you have established for your folks, but should also incorporate all of the other unique skills that your players have developed over their years of preparation. Some managers (which are vastly different animals than leaders) attempt to rigidly confine contributions from team members to purely formal roles, but leaders of championship teams know that the total truly exceeds the sum of the parts only when they allow their players to use *all* available skills to help the team win.

Football coaches do this extremely well. Beyond the specialization between players I mentioned previously, there's a second layer of specialization that coaches exploit to the team's advantage during the game. Some defensive tackles are extremely good at rushing the quarterback during passing plays, while other defensive tackles are terrific at crushing running backs during running plays. These are two different (but related) talents belonging to different players who play the same position, and coaches take advantage of this natural differentiation. In fact, they depend on it. During situations in which the opposing team is more likely to pass than run, coaches ensure their best pass rushers are on the field. In running situations, coaches put in their ace run stoppers. The different players fill the same positions on the field, but the team benefits from diverse skill sets as the situation dictates. You should make use of your team's varied talents in the same way.

"Find the one thing in your heart that drives you to be great. It may be your faith, your family, or your friends. Hold on to it, and draw strength from it when times get tough."
~ *Chris Valletta*

Game day is the opportunity for your team to enjoy the fruits of their labors. As their leader, you can help your champion players stay confident and relaxed in the moments before the big event by expressing your pride in their preparation and your confidence in their abilities. Teaching your players to use the same self-mastery techniques that keep you poised and present in the moment, rather than burning stomach acid with worry over a future problem that may never materialize, will help your team members perform at their best when unexpected challenges crop up. Finally, encouraging your team to use every one of their talents – not just those that happen to fall narrowly in their job description – will help your team work together seamlessly to solve challenges using the right expertise. If you do these things well, you'll soon be celebrating one victory after another.

Team WORKS! – Chapter 9

Celebrate Like a Champion

Savor your victory, honor your players, and get back to work!

If you're following the playbook as you recruit, hire, train, and field your championship business team, and if your team's game day execution is focused, prepared, and relaxed, you're going to rack up a ton of wins. It's time to talk about how to handle all those victories!

I've been on many successful teams over the years in both sports and business, and I have been privileged to enjoy many big wins. I've seen teams celebrate exceptionally well, and emerge from their victory - and from their victory celebration - stronger and better than before. I've also seen the "never-ending celebration" phenomenon destroy talented teams.

You've built your championship team to last, and while you should savor every victory your team achieves, you need to inculcate the mindset that victory is, in fact, *business as usual* on your team. So you need to be deliberate about how you celebrate your victories in order to keep achieving them, and you need to keep a close eye on the way your team responds to a big win.

I can hear the skeptics: "You're kidding, right? You're going to teach us how to *celebrate*?" You're absolutely right I am, because done poorly, celebration leads to lack of preparation for your next big test. In fact, the way you and your players celebrate a victory reveals a great deal about the fundamental quality and character of your team.

Here's what I mean. If you're a true champion, you're not in the game just for a trophy. True champions compete because they love the process of becoming ever-better in their chosen field, they love the game they play, and they love the strength, character, and integrity they gain through the process of striving for excellence.

Teams who are just in it to achieve a goal often do just that – they achieve *one* big goal, and then recede back into mediocrity and obscurity. Their players and coaches are able to make sacrifices just long enough to reach an arbitrary (though obviously worthy) goal, but they consume themselves in the process.

Suddenly, once they achieve their goal, they're far less willing to continue making the same sacrifices that brought them victory.

What separates dynasties and legends from one-hit wonders is the love of the *process* of excellence. For champions with staying power, striving for excellence isn't consuming or exhausting; instead, it's energizing. At the end of a long day of hard work doing something I love, I don't feel tired - I feel fantastic! In fact, I'm often disappointed that the day is over so quickly. On the other hand, if I'm stuck doing things I don't enjoy, the days feel endless and every milestone feels as though it has shortened my lifespan. Doing what you love is the only way to live your life well, and it's the only way to attain enduring greatness in your field. Sacrificing yourself on the altar of "success" is the well-worn path to burnout.

Note that the important difference between the path to greatness and the path to burnout doesn't relate to the specific tasks you perform in order to win. Rather, the difference is entirely in the way you and your players approach what you're doing. If you love your work, you will enjoy mastering the Little Things. If you view the Little Things only as a means to an end, they will sap your energy (and you won't do them nearly as well as you would if you enjoyed them). But the Little Things themselves haven't changed.

Why am I spending time on this in a chapter on celebration? Because the way your team performs in the weeks after a big win will tell you whether you need to make personnel changes. You might even find that you have to replace one of your standout players, as it's often only after a big victory that you'll know for sure what motivates your team members. As I mentioned in Chapter 4, the kind of players you'll need to find and keep in order to put together a truly spectacular business team are the ones who love what they do on a daily basis. You're not interested in keeping the players who just grit their teeth and put up with discomfort long enough to chalk up a big win or two – even if they happen to be incredibly talented. As we saw, the "best" players aren't always the right players for your team, and if your team members are not in the game because they love the game itself, watch out. Your first big victory may be your last.

A player's love for the game can also diminish over time, and you'll need to keep an eye out for this problem as well. It manifests itself in the same way: you'll notice reduced effort, lower standards, and less engagement.

This happens all the time, and there are plenty of examples of high-quality athletes and teams whose preparation declined precipitously after a big win. Mike Tyson, the youngest heavy-weight champion in boxing history, famous for his devastating knockout victories, rested on his laurels after a number of impressive triumphs - only to walk into a knockout punch thrown by an unknown upstart named Buster Douglas.

In 2004, the New York Yankees charged to a 3-game lead over the Boston Red Sox in the American League Championship Series, and came within three outs of earning a trip to the World Series of baseball. Perhaps the Yanks began celebrating too soon, however, as they subsequently fell completely apart, dismantling their big lead through mental mistakes and lack of focus. Boston went on to win both the American League and the World Series championships.

My Alma Mater, Texas A&M, took a lackadaisical approach to their preparation to face a perennially weak Baylor team in 2004. The Aggies kept celebrating their big overtime win against Colorado when they should have been focusing on the Little Things that would help them beat Baylor in the next game. As a result, A&M suffered its first lost to the Bears in 25 years. The demoralizing defeat was costly, and was the turning point for the entire season as the Aggies lost three out of the next four games.

Regardless of talent and expertise, no team or player is immune to the effects of a post-victory malaise. Michael Jordan, undoubtedly the greatest basketball player in NBA history, and one of history's best professional athletes in any sport, knew this better than anyone. He said, "Somewhere out there, someone is working harder than me, and someday I will meet that person head-on. If they've outworked me, I will lose." Did Michael celebrate his many championship victories and individual MVP accolades? Absolutely! But he celebrated like a champion, in order to *remain* a champion. Your job as the player-coach of your world-class business team is to ensure that your players do the same.

It's a three-step process: celebrate hard, recognize your players, and *get back to work*! That's how the dominant sports franchises do business – the Pittsburgh Steelers of the 1970s, the San Francisco 49ers of the 1980s, the Dallas Cowboys of the 1990s, and the New England Patriots of the 2000s all racked up championship after championship by applying this process. I think it will work for your team, too.

"I celebrate a victory when I start walking off the field. By the time I get to the locker room, I'm done."
~ Tom Osborne, 1973-1997 Nebraska University Head Football Coach

Tom Osborne's philosophy may be a bit extreme – he's known for celebrating his victories only during the walk off of the field – but the perennial champions I listed above, and my own championship teams, use a mindset similar to his. Tom allocates a finite period of time to thoroughly enjoy a big win, and then he gets right back to the business of continually striving for greatness. His celebrations were a bit shorter and more low-key than mine usually are, but there is deep wisdom in his approach, and here is how I implement it in my business team.

Immediately after a big success, I gather my players together for a quick word of congratulations, and I also announce the location of the *real* celebration that will follow, complete with food and libations. Families are invited to share in the joy, because their efforts at home enable my players to show up to work ready and focused every day. I make it clear to everyone that our big win is a big deal, and we're going to enjoy it in a big way.

When the celebration kicks off in earnest, I let my team relive great moments from the big event, share laughs, and talk through the narrowly averted near-catastrophes that are always part of both business and sports. There is a lot of laughter and cheer, and I take great joy in watching my players relish a big win. I also love celebrating right along with them!

At some point during the celebration, I take the floor to say a few words. You won't be surprised to hear that my victory speech is almost exactly the same as my pregame speech: I thank my players for all of the effort and time that went into preparing for the big event, congratulate them on achieving fantastic results, and express my pride in their professionalism, dedication, and talent.

I take it one step further, though, and I go out of my way to recognize my star performers. I cite specific examples of how individual contributions and clutch performances helped vault the team to victory, and I hand out awards to commemorate individual contributions to the team's victory. As we saw in Chapter 7, recognizing and reinforcing positive practices is fundamental to building and maintaining a championship team, and lauding your team members in front of their friends and family is a critically important leadership practice.

A word of caution, however: I think it's important to prepare your recognition remarks in advance. I'm not suggesting that you should read a speech – you absolutely should NOT read from a script, as everything you say must come straight from your gut – but I am saying that you need to carefully consider the contributions of your entire team in order to make sure you don't unintentionally leave someone out. If you recognize most of your team members' contributions but accidentally leave out a few key performers, you'll run the risk of fostering ill will and resentment. So think about each player on your team (for large organizations, it makes more sense to address each division instead of each individual), jot down on a note card the things you appreciate most about their involvement, and reference your notes as you address your team at the victory celebration.

I wrap up my **brief** comments by laying out the time frame for our celebration. It's absolutely essential to let your team know that you want them to thoroughly and completely enjoy themselves, but for a limited amount of time. I let them know in no uncertain terms that they have earned the right to celebrate, but that we'll soon be back to work earning the right to enjoy our next victory. "My heartfelt thanks for all of your efforts," I might say. "Savor this moment – you've earned it. Take Monday off to spend time with your family and unwind, and let's all show up on Tuesday with our work boots and hard hats on. We'll need to be rested and ready to tackle the Hanzelka deal."

"I'll rest when I'm dead."
~ Coach JB Grimes, Chris's Offensive Line Coach at Texas A&M responding to the question of whether he would rest after the big win against Nebraska in 1998.

What happens when everyone shows up to work after the celebration period is over? Absolutely the same things that happened before the big win – we seek perfection in the Little Things, review our previous performance, reinforce positive events, and troubleshoot miscues. In short, we get back to business as usual, which is to say we continue the passionate pursuit of greatness.

The recognition and reinforcement don't stop after the post-game gathering. I follow the example set by icons like Lou Holtz, Bobby Bowden, and Bill Gates: I recognize top performers formally once we get back to work, either at a company-wide meeting, with bulletin board notices, in company-wide emails, or all of the above.

I do this for two reasons: first, I really am grateful for their performance, and I want to make sure the honor is worthy of the honoree. Second, as we saw in Chapter 7, public recognition supplies a source of motivation for everyone else to improve their own performance. My championship teams are full of driven, competitive all-stars, and each one of them wants to achieve great things. Seeing their coworker's picture in the "MVP" plaque on the wall makes them silently think, "*I* want to put together an MVP performance!"

I learned how effective recognition can be from legendary coach RC Slocum. During my redshirt year at A&M, I was on the scout team, responsible for playing the role of the opponent during the week's practices to help the varsity defense prepare for the upcoming game. Each week, during the last meeting before the game that we had prepped the starters to play, Coach Slocum would give out the "Look Award." The Look Award went to the scout team player who gave the best "look" to the starters. In other words, if I was playing the role of the starting guard for the Oklahoma Sooners that week, it was my job to provide the starting defensive tackle for A&M with the most realistic representation of his upcoming opponent's style and technique that I possibly could. It was incumbent upon me to watch film of the Oklahoma player and emulate his method and manner as perfectly as possible.

Week after week, all I wanted was to win that award, to show everyone that I was a ball player. I quickly realized that I had some serious competition, worthy of a full Division 1 scholarship like mine. I battled hard, and when I finally won the Look Award (it took me 4 weeks), I was both elated and even more motivated. My objective became to win another Look Award, and another, and another after that. I wasn't alone in this drive for recognition, as my cohorts all fought hard to be the week's best scout team player. Coach Slocum's accolades fostered a competitive attitude of improvement and excellence, and it paid off in spades. We were a terrific scout team, and it helped our varsity team immensely on game day.

In addition to celebrating the larger victories in business, such as landing a new account or contract, a merger, going public, or earning a new round of funding, it's important to also celebrate the smaller successes along the way to the big wins. I do this in a more informal way. For example, one of my favorite pastimes is listening to my sales reps recount the events that led to closing a deal of any size. I love it when they relive the moments leading up to hearing "yes" from the client. It's similar to the scenes in the movie "Glengarry Glen Ross" (my favorite movie of all time) where the salesmen tell colorful stories of their most recent sales pitches, and I love seeing my team members in their element and reveling in the moment. In addition to providing great motivation for everyone, the rest of my sales team usually learns a new tactic, technique or strategy by listening to what works for others on the team.

> *"You're never as good as everyone tells you when you win, and you're never as bad as they say when you lose."*
> ~ *Lou Holtz, National Champion Football Coach, Notre Dame*

What happens on those rare occasions when things don't go quite as well as we had hoped? You might be surprised to learn that very little changes about my post-game approach. I still gather my team and their families together, express my pride and gratitude, acknowledge terrific contributions, and celebrate the many kernels of greatness in our effort.

"So you're celebrating defeat?" you might ask. Not even close.

I hate defeat. But it's part of life in business and athletics, so I use it to my advantage. My team is full of world-class players who take great pride in their work, and they hate losing just as much as I do. It falls to me as their leader to put the disappointing outcome in its proper perspective, and my job is still – always – to reinforce positive aspects of my team's performance. I accomplish those things in largely the same way after a defeat as I do following an important victory.

> *If you can react the same way to winning and losing, that's a*
> *big accomplishment.*
> *~ Chris Evert Lloyd*

Obviously, the mood at our post-game gathering isn't terribly jubilant if the proverbial clock ran out on us while the other team had more points, but I still bring my team members and their families out to let off steam, bandage the wounds of defeat, and build upon the positive parts of our performance. It's even more important to recognize great contributions after a defeat, so I make sure I'm very thorough as I thank my team members for their effort.

I don't do any analysis whatsoever at this post-game gathering. We're professionals, and professionals always dissect their previous performances to glean insights for improvement. But we do that at the proper time: after we get back to work. Like most high achievers, my players begin analyzing their own performance the nanosecond after the clock runs out. I use the post-game gathering to make sure that as they ruminate on the loss, they do so with the right focus and a sanguine perspective. Otherwise, it's easy for them to become discouraged and overly-critical, which can lead to a performance slump.

My closing remarks at the post-game event aren't much different than after a victory: "Thank you for pouring your hearts into this event. I'm proud of your effort, and it's an honor to be associated with you. Let's enjoy this time together, and let's all show up on Monday focused and ready to get back to work on the Little Things."

Disappointing outcomes are inevitable on the path to greatness, and mastering your mindset in the face of defeat can feel challenging. But champions make the most of the opportunity for growth, and use defeat to stoke the fire of excellence. World-class leaders take extra care to reinforce positive aspects of their team's efforts, highlight standout performances, and help put their players in the right frame of mind to get back to the Little Things in earnest.

"When I lose, I'm boiling inside. I just try not to show it because it's a lack of composure, and if you give in to your emotions after one loss, you're liable to have three or four in a row."
~ Chris Evert Loyd

Unlike the one-win wonders, true champions celebrate their victories, learn from their mistakes, and quickly get back to work on the Little Things in preparation for the next big test. Lead your team's victory celebration by expressing your pride in their efforts, recognizing great performances, and clearly setting your expectations for when and how your players will start preparing for the next challenge. When things don't quite go your way, guide your championship team through the disappointment of defeat by acknowledging and reinforcing great contributions, putting the loss in the right perspective, and building on the positives to show up better prepared for victory in the next game. Stack your team with players who love the process of attaining and maintaining excellence, and celebrate their successes even in defeat. You and your team will soon be enjoying victory after victory!

Team WORKS! – Chapter 10

The Secret Ingredient: Rope-Holders

A winning team is made up of 100% Rope-Holders. 99% won't cut it.

Everything we've talked about so far in this book has been absolutely essential and unequivocally necessary in order to build a championship business team. But the attributes, attitudes, strategies, and techniques we've discussed to this point are not, by themselves, *sufficient* to produce a world-class team.

Way back in Chapter 4, when I gave you my list of important attributes to look for in your championship business team members, I also told you that I was saving one key characteristic for last. I also mentioned that this particular quality isn't just any old nice-to-have quality to cultivate on your team - it is the one element that will make or break your entire effort.

The time has come for the rest of the story.

In 1994, just before my sophomore year in high school, my family moved from New Hampshire to Plano, Texas. I walked into an environment that was, on all levels, light-years ahead of my quaint New Hampshire experience. My new peers were far more academically, physically, and mentally mature than I was. I had been a big fish in a small pond in my East Coast town, but my new Texas classmates and teammates seemed to have left me in the dust.

My first day of football practice was eye-opening. The players in Texas were so much different than my teammates in New Hampshire. While my former teammates clearly cared about their performance on the gridiron, my new Texas cohorts were extremely determined and driven. It was clear to me from the way they approached every drill that being a member of their football team came with significant responsibility. They were serious, motivated, and relentless. I was by far the largest and most athletic kid on the field at 6'3" and 285 lbs. (and I'm pretty sure I was the only kid my size who could dunk a basketball), but I was intimidated by my new teammates' intensity, focus, and skill.

My teammates' strong sense of accountability to the team isn't without just cause. Plano High School has one of the most storied high-school football programs in the country, and each player on the team felt privileged to have the opportunity to play for such a strong program. They also felt the enormous weight of extremely high expectations, and nobody wanted to let the program down. This would undoubtedly be true of any successful high school football program in any state, but it was doubly so in Texas, where high school football ranks just behind oxygen, food, and the Church on the list of life priorities.

How big is Texas high school football? Big enough that Plano Senior High School has an indoor football practice facility. At the time, neither my college team, perennial powerhouse Texas A&M, nor my second pro team, the New Orleans Saints, boasted an indoor practice facility, yet it's business as usual for a Texas high school program to enjoy climate-controlled practices.

My performance during the first football practice at my new high school was absolutely unremarkable. I was the biggest, strongest, and most athletic player on the team, but I was tentative and intimidated by my new environment. My performance didn't water anyone's eyes, and I did my best to blend in. If there was such a thing as a "big league" high school football program, this was it, and I wasn't sure I had what it took to carve a spot on the roster. I didn't want to highlight myself in a negative way, so I didn't highlight myself at all.

It was at that first practice that I met the person who would change the direction of my path in football, business, and life. His name was Mike Hughes, and at the time he was the offensive line coach for Plano Senior High School. Coach Hughes was tough, strong, uncompromising, and extremely sharp. He knew football better than anyone I'd ever met.

He began our working relationship with a shot across the bow. Mike brought me into his office after my tepid performance in the first practice session, looked me square in the eye, and said, "Son, if you want to be on my offensive line, then you are going to have become a rope-holder. I don't care how big, strong, fast, and athletic you are. If you aren't a rope-holder, then there is no room for you on this team." I had no idea what he was talking about, but it sounded fairly important to him.

Little did I know, I had just been introduced to the concept that would become the centerpiece of my life and business philosophy.

To understand what Coach Hughes meant, imagine yourself hanging off of the side of a cliff by a rope. A rocky bluff waits a thousand feet beneath you, and above you, at the other end of your rope, stands one person - your rope-holder. Who do you want holding your rope? What qualities must your rope-holder possess?

Strength, obviously, is a prerequisite. But so are perseverance, steadfastness, commitment, and mountains of mental toughness. Strong arms without a strong mind are useless as soon as fatigue and discomfort begin to set in; likewise, all the courage in the world won't overcome the absence of the basic physical tools to do the job – in our metaphor, the job of saving you from a thousand-foot fall to your death. You want your rope-holder to be the perfect blend of physical ability and mental tenacity, equal parts grit, gumption, guts, and guns.

In extreme circumstances, rope-holders rise to the occasion. They seem to have an extra reserve of energy, strength, resiliency, and willpower that allows them to achieve incredible things and put forth herculean effort when it counts most.

No event better encapsulates what it means to me to be a rope-holder than the tragic collapse of the Texas A&M bonfire in the fall of 1999. It was tradition that every year in advance of the football game against our arch-nemesis, the University of Texas, A&M students constructed a gigantic, 50+ Foot bonfire. It was built of thousands of wooden logs, and constructing the structure took months of effort by students and volunteers. The bonfire was traditionally lit in a ceremony a night or two before the Texas game.

Tragically, in the early morning hours on November 18th, as 58 volunteers continued their round-the-clock effort to complete the structure in time for the next week's festivities, the support wires gave way. Five thousand logs, stacked six stories high, collapsed in a matter of seconds. Dozens of students became trapped beneath tons of wood. Some died instantly, and others suffered horrible injuries.

When we caught wind of the collapse early that morning, the entire football team rushed to the site. Because there were still people trapped alive in the rubble, officials were unable to use heavy equipment to remove the logs, and volunteers were struggling to lift the massive logs off of the pile, one by one. My teammates and I immediately began to help, carrying as many logs off the pile as we could. We labored for hours alongside our classmates, witnessing grisly scenes of death and dismemberment while working to exhaustion to remove the logs from atop the remaining survivors as quickly as possible. We didn't stop for rest and we barely paused for breath. The logs were large and heavy, and we pushed ourselves beyond what we thought to be our limits. But along with the rest of the rope-holders working to rescue our friends and classmates, we never thought twice about the struggle. We knew they were counting on us, and we rose to the occasion.

The football game against Texas a few days later was another rope-holder moment. My teammates and I felt as though we had the opportunity to honor the victims and their families; more than that, we felt that we represented them on an incredibly large stage. The tragic events galvanized the Aggie nation of former students and fans, and we faced an extremely tough Texas team – ranked #5 in the nation – in front of 90,000 fans and a national television audience. It was a huge moment for our team, and we felt a sense of purpose that was much deeper than the one that accompanied a normal football game.

We were well prepared, well coached, and extremely motivated, but it was a brutally tough game. I vividly recall moments of nearly debilitating exhaustion during the game. My head swum, I found myself gasping for breath, and my arms and legs burned. After a particularly long and exhausting play, I was so drained that I began to doubt whether I could continue. But I looked around me and noticed that all ten of my teammates in the huddle were just as fatigued as I was. We were in rough shape, and barely hanging on – in front of the largest audience in memory.

But something seemed to change for us in that moment. We stepped beyond ourselves and our mental limits. We stopped focusing on our burning lungs and dead-weight legs, and became cognizant once again of our shared commitment to winning what we felt was the biggest game we had ever played. We remembered that our friends and teammates were counting on us, and we rallied.

Like the rope-holders we were, we rose to the occasion. At the end of a tragic and deeply emotional week, we transcended our own limits to upset the Longhorns.

Being a rope-holder sometimes involves a transcendent instantaneous effort like our victory over Texas, but it also involves a steady, day-in and day-out commitment to the team's goals. In a business context, a rope-holder is dedicated to the team's vision and goals for the long term. Without this team focus, all the talent, strength, courage, and mental toughness in the world won't make any difference. Teams are comprised of individuals, but championship teams only form when the life goals and daily practices of its individuals intertwine seamlessly with the team's objectives.

It isn't that the individuals on a world-class crew sacrifice themselves for the team; "sacrifice" is the kind of empty and short-lived dedication that is really a form of manipulation, as it is almost always tied to expectations of a reward. Instead, championship teams recruit, hire, train, and retain the players who love doing the things that are good for the team, *for the sake of the doing*. Rope-holders can always be counted on to work for the good of the team because it is in their nature to do so. In other words, the work that rope-holders love to do is also the work that propels the team forward.

A rope-holder, in short, is someone you and the rest of your team can trust. They'll be there when you need them. They have the physical, mental, and emotional tools to hold their share of the rope's load, and they have the constitution and shared vision to continue contributing to the team's goals when times get rough. They have the perfect combination of aptitude and attitude. Rope-holders have your back, every time.

Coach Hughes' comments to me in his office after my first practice in Plano began a years-long lesson in teamwork, leadership, and excellence. Mike's instruction and object lessons helped distill the art and science of teamwork into a single, all-encompassing unified theory of successful teams: unless your team is made up of rope-holders, you don't have a winning team. Your team can boast all of the talent in the world, but if it isn't comprised entirely of rope-holders, it will come apart at the seams.

"When I check your references, you might earn the T.R.U. & S... If you want to earn the final "T," then let's go to war together."
~ Coach Tom Osborne during Chris Valletta's recruiting visit to the University of Nebraska

Coach Tom Osborne echoed Mike Hughes' priceless rope-holder lesson on my recruiting trip to Lincoln, Nebraska. He taught me that the rumor mill, references, game tape, and my reputation could get me in the door, but if I wanted his full trust, then I had to prove myself on the field. There is no better way to figure out whether you can trust an individual than to go to battle with them by your side.

On the gridiron, I knew immediately if I could trust and depend on the man next to me. Would he remember his assignments? Would he make the right calls? I vividly remember playing a game where the lineman next to me had absolutely no idea what he was doing. He was the most physically talented player on the offensive line, but he had never dedicated himself to making the most of his ability. His forgotten assignments and missed calls diminished my abilities as a player as well, because I couldn't rely on him to be where I needed him. Playing next to him made *me* worse! It wasn't until the coach replaced him with a less talented but more trustworthy player that our offensive line became a cohesive unit.

Trust brings out the best in every team, but it only arises when each player is trust*worthy*. When your players or employees are all on the same page, know their responsibilities, and have the skill and courage to execute without hesitation, your team will have what it takes to rise to championship form.

It might sound somewhat trivial to say that it's important to recruit, hire, train, and field a team full of people you can trust – after all, who would do otherwise? But a surprising number of businesses fall short of filling their teams with rope-holders. Or, more accurately, the vast majority of businesses fail to foster a rope-holder culture, and they don't actively screen their prospective and existing team members for rope-holder attributes. Why? Because it's not all that easy to figure out who is a rope-holder and who isn't. It takes time and testing.

It isn't that their hiring and vetting processes aren't thorough. Many companies institute a very lengthy and exhaustive hiring process. Nor is the problem that their training programs aren't comprehensive, as many companies put together extensive onboarding events.

The problem is that most business teams don't recruit, train, and develop their players with the right objectives in mind. Most business teams focus solely on cultivating job skills and enforcing the ubiquitous list of employee conduct rules, and never really get to the heart of what makes a successful team.

As the leader of your championship team, you won't make the same mistake. Over the course of the previous chapters, I've given you the framework to discover and develop the right set of skill sets in your players in order to field a world class business team. Now, we're going to complete the picture by adding the crucial last dimension, the ongoing and uncompromising development of a pervasive, rock-solid rope-holder culture.

Developing a team full of rope-holders won't require you to modify any of the strategies and tactics that I've given you in previous chapters, as each of the attributes you'll foster by following the playbook I've laid out for you are crucial aspects of your rope-holders' skill set and mentality.

In fact, following the playbook is the only way to discover whether your promising hires are rope-holder material. That's because rope-holders only reveal themselves through time and trial. Even though you'll spend a great deal of time and energy hiring people you believe will be the right players for your championship team, and not just the most talented or credentialed players available, you'll never be 100% positive at the time you make the hiring decision that you've found a true rope-holder.

You've crafted a world-class redshirt program to mature and develop your players prior to putting them in the game, and this process is not just to improve their skills and knowledge. It is also an opportunity for you to observe your new hires in an environment that's unfamiliar to them, and probably a bit stressful. With each day that passes and each task your redshirts accomplish on the way to graduation from your training program, they will reveal more about their character and fortitude. You and the rest of your team will also begin to get a better sense of how well the new players are likely to fit in, and you'll gain a better understanding of your new team members' work ethic, drive, and willingness to pitch in. The redshirt program is the second step on your journey to discovering whether your new folks are rope-holder material.

"Courage is resistance to fear, mastery of fear - not absence of fear."
~ Mark Twain

Once your new hires graduate from your redshirt program and begin their daily work on your team, you'll really start to see what they're made of. The pressure of daily performance will further reveal their character, and you and the rest of your team will get a far better sense of their aptitude and attitude. The honeymoon phase will soon end, and any residual pre-hiring façade – which is an inevitable part of being human and wanting to put your best self forward into a new employment situation - will fade away over time to reveal more and more of your new players' constitution.

Watch this process carefully, as you will often only discover what may be serious incompatibilities well after your new team members have been all the way through your hiring process and graduated from your redshirt program. In order to build a rock-solid rope-holder culture on your championship business team, you will need to pay constant attention to the way your players reveal themselves over time.

As time passes, your team will encounter important situations with high stakes, and your new team members will be called on to perform at a championship level. These moments are critical not just because there are important business outcomes on the line, but also because you can only form an accurate understanding of how your team members handle pressure by observing them when the chips are down. Does your tall, fast, talented receiver drop passes when the game is on the line? Does your rocket-arm quarterback lose his cool when the clock starts to wind down? Does your silver-tongued salesman get tongue-tied in a Fortune 500 boardroom? Does your new CMO become a tyrant in the face of a looming deadline? You'll never know beforehand.

I'm not insinuating that rope-holders never make mistakes or come up short. Rope-holders come through with flying colors on the vast majority of occasions – that's why you combed the earth looking for their rare combination of talent and character – but they reveal the more fallible side of their humanity on occasion as well.

Your job is to watch two things: how often your team members come up short, and how they respond *after* their mistakes. Rope-holders must be trustworthy, which means that they must earn your unfaltering confidence. Occasional errors happen to even the best players on the planet, but talented players who repeatedly commit mental errors or frequently suffer from concentration lapses aren't rope-holder material. It might be difficult, but it's best to let them go.

"It is in times of trial when some men are broken and some men rise up. What type of man are you?"
~ Chris Valletta

Rope-holders don't fall apart after a mistake, either. They obviously feel deeply disappointed about miscues, but truly trustworthy team members don't further jeopardize the team by remaining in a mental and emotional funk after a mistake. They accept full responsibility for their slip-up, but the error doesn't continue to reverberate in their skull, which would take their mind off of the important task at hand *right now*. True rope-holders examine what went wrong, implement the necessary changes to improve their performance, and focus their full attention on the next task.

Rope-holders never shirk responsibility. Players are only trustworthy if they hold themselves personally and publicly accountable for their performance. A player who points fingers at other teammates without fully facing his own culpability has no place on a championship team. Let him go – he's a great candidate for your competitor's team!

I'm not advocating a "one strike" approach. Developing into a rope-holder is often an evolutionary process, and it takes judgment and maturity on your part as the team leader to afford your players the latitude to learn from their errors – even their serious ones – and continuously improve their performance and their character. This is particularly true of your younger team members, who must often experience more than a few gaffes as they grow into themselves.

How many mistakes are too many? Every situation is different. One crime is enough for a jail sentence, and you shouldn't tolerate an egregious breach of your business' principles and values. On the other hand, talented players with outstanding attitudes have bad days, experience difficult personal situations, and go through slumps. Your job as the team leader is to gather the salient facts, seek to fully understand all sides of the issue, and act decisively in the best interest of your team and your players. Most often, your superstars will correct their own mistakes and bounce back better than ever. Only occasionally will you feel the need to step in, but when you do take action, do it with commitment.

Green Bay Packers head coach Mike Holmgren tolerated more than a few boneheaded mistakes from a promising young quarterback on his roster. Mike had to control his own anger and disappointment on many occasions as the young man went through countless personal and athletic growth pains, often with serious consequences for the rest of the team. But under Mike's guidance, the promising young athlete always bounced back, worked hard, owned up to his errors, and demanded excellence of himself. His name was Brett Favre, and in addition to rewriting the NFL record books, Brett went on to lead the Packers to two conference championships and a Super Bowl victory.

Mike Holmgren's patience and persistence paid off, but he didn't place his trust in Brett blindly. Brett proved that he was rope-holder material through his character and work ethic. Favre worked hard to live up to his coach's expectations, and over time, Holmgren led the young quarterback to greatness. The Packers' experience demonstrates that cultivating a rope-holder culture can be a tumultuous process, but if you follow the playbook, you'll experience championship results of your own.

"The good news is that everyone is trustworthy. The bad news is that we're short, slow, and not nearly as athletic as the rest of the teams in our district!"
~ High School Football Coach before the start of his team's first undefeated season in 10 years

Coach Mike Hughes and my high school teammates did something very similar for me during my time on the Plano Senior High School offensive line. They immersed me in a rope-holder environment, and I began to emulate the other players' attitudes and grow into my role as a contributing member of a championship team. I started working harder than I ever had before so that I wouldn't let my team down. I started to gain respect among my peers because I fought tooth and nail for my team, and over time I proved through my work ethic and steady play that I was a trustworthy part of their top tier team. Slowly, I became like the people that I had been emulating. I woke up one day and realized that I had finally become a rope-holder!

It was great for my team, as they had gained a new rock-steady contributor, but through the unselfish attitude of being a rope-holder, amazing things also started happening to my career. I became the most recruited offensive lineman in the country. I was offered over 115 college scholarships to play football across the country. I made every all conference, all area, all district, all state, and All-American team that there was to make. Because of my attitude towards my team, amazing things happened to me personally. Mike Hughes' philosophy was truly life changing!

"Give me a business team of people who are passionate, driven, and nothing but rope-holders, and I'll show you a business that's successful beyond measure."
~ Chris Valletta

Developing a team full of rope-holders is a never-ending process. It pervades everything you do, and underlies every decision you make. It never happens overnight, which is another way of saying that you're going to have to have the strength of will and character to persevere right along with your players as they - *and you* - grow into rope-holders.

That's right. We've come full-circle, and the process of building a championship business team has led us right back to you, your character, your work ethic, and your integrity. You gather rope-holders around you only by being a rope-holder yourself. You have no prayer of attracting, keeping, or leading a team of talented, trustworthy players unless you personify the values you seek in them. You must *be* what you seek in your players. Your team will only ever be what *you* are. Your team will never exceed your example.

Want a team full of skilled, sharp, relentless superstars? You must be one yourself. Want a team characterized by deep resilience and unwavering dedication? Those qualities must reside at the center of you. Want a team full of players who look out for each other, support each other, and build each other up? You must do those things.

It bears repeating: your team will never surpass your example. To lead a championship business team comprised of 100% rope-holders, you must exemplify what it means to be a rope-holder yourself.

That's all there is to it.

Building a championship business team isn't rocket science or brain surgery, but it requires every bit of your heart and soul. This playbook has given you the time-tested tools, tactics, techniques, and strategies to develop your own world class business team. I've given you a rock-solid formula for developing a team full of trustworthy, talented team players. They are the very same strategies that I employ every day on my championship teams, and the values of integrity, discipline, and character infuse every successful team I've ever been associated with.

Use these values and strategies as your guideposts. Be relentless in your pursuit of becoming the perfect rope-holder. Surround yourself with people who share your passion for excellence, trustworthiness, and team success. Recruit, train, and retain the right players, and not just the "best" players. Above all, exemplify the qualities you want for your team: be patient, passionate, trustworthy, and committed.

If you do these things, you will surely develop a championship business team. I guarantee it!

Afterword

By Coach Mike Hughes

I first met Chris and his family in the spring of 1994 when they moved to Plano, Texas. It took some time, but Chris Valletta became one of the best high school football players I've ever coached. What set Chris apart from the other players? Well, being 6'3" and 280 pounds didn't hurt, but more importantly it was the work ethic that he developed and that burning desire to be the best.

I started coaching football in 1979 as an assistant coach. I was very fortunate to have worked under Head Coach Tommy Kimbrough for several years at Plano Senior High. In 2002, a dream came true for me when I became the Head Coach and Athletic Director at Plano West Senior High School. The day I was hired I set out to build not only a winning program, but one of the top high school programs in the state of Texas, and I'm laying the foundation to make that a reality. It's no different than building a winning team in business.

How do I do it or where do I start? One of the first things that I set out to do was surround myself with good assistant coaches, but more importantly, good people—people I could count on, people who were loyal, and people who cared about kids. Chris calls it "finding the *right* people."

The second thing I focused on was a "we-not-me" attitude. Everything that we do at Plano West Senior High is centered on the team. It's no different in the business world. Put the team first, and good things will happen. If you have a bunch of individuals going in different directions, each with a private agenda, get ready to get beat.

Third, our players know that we care about them. If your employees know that you care about them as well, then the sky is the limit.

The last chapter in Chris's book, "Rope-Holders" is my favorite because I know Chris got the idea from me. I used this saying quite often when he played for me. I would ask my players "Are you a rope-holder? If I were hanging off the side of a cliff by a rope and you were holding the other end, could I count on you?"

Chris is absolutely right: a winning team is made up of 100% rope-holders.

Mike Hughes
Head Coach/Athletic Director
Plano West Senior High School
Plano, Texas

About the Author

At the age of 12, Chris Valletta's Dad gave him a birthday present he'd never forget: center court, floor seats at the Boston Garden to watch Larry Bird and the Boston Celtics take on Michael Jordan and the Chicago Bulls. To a kid whose room looked more like a Michael Jordan shrine than a bedroom, it was a dream come true. There was only one problem. On the day before the game, Chris was diagnosed with chicken pox, and he couldn't go to the game. At home in front of the TV, through tears of disappointment, Chris watched Jordan have an epic night, lighting up the Celtics with a 40+ point performance.

Determined, he set out on a course that would seem a bit insane: "If I can't watch him play, I'm going to play against him," Valletta said. Chris immersed himself into the game of basketball, becoming one of the best players in the state. He was selected to the prestigious Amateur Athletic Union team, and represented his state in the national tournament. At 15 years old and already 6'2" tall, it seemed as if the dream of playing against Jordan was becoming a bit more tangible.

There was only one issue: Chris also weighed 260 pounds, and the football coaches were drooling over the potential of a 15 year old lineman with college-ready size and great athleticism at such a young age. It didn't take long for Chris to realize that the game of basketball was actually preparing him to become one of the most talented offensive linemen in the country.

While Chris was learning footwork and teamwork in athletics, he was also learning leadership and business acumen from his father. In between Chris's many athletic events, which he never missed, John Valletta was busy climbing the corporate ranks, rising to become President of Super 8 and Howard Johnson Hotels. Chris learned a great deal about building championship business teams during many dinner conversations over the years.

After winning two high-school state football championships, Chris accepted a scholarship to Division I powerhouse Texas A&M University, where he became a four-year letterman under legendary coach R.C. Slocum, the winningest coach in Texas A&M history. During Chris's tenure, the Aggies won both the Big XII South Championship in 1997 and the Big XII Championship in 1998. After earning degrees in Speech Communication/ Rhetoric and Political Science, Chris went on to a career in the NFL with the Tennessee Titans and New Orleans Saints, finishing his career as a member of the eventual 2002 Super Bowl Champion Tampa Bay Buccaneers under first-year coach Jon Gruden.

Chris retired from the NFL at age 23 and moved to Dallas, TX where he launched his entrepreneurial career. By day, Chris worked as an advertising sales executive. He broke a 79-year company record by generating $2 million in new revenue in his first year. By night, Chris launched his first company, a real estate firm specializing in transacting residential properties using electronic media outlets like eBay. Chris's new company transacted over 20 residential properties with values in excess of $4 million in the first year.

The success of the real estate business quickly caught the attention of billionaire real estate mogul Donald Trump, who selected Chris from a pool of over one million applicants to be a contestant for the hit NBC reality show *The Apprentice, Season 4*. It was clear from the beginning that Chris's understanding of the successful inner workings of an athletic team translated to the business environment with perfect synergy.

Chris sold his real estate firm in 2005, and moved to New York City to join fellow entrepreneur and Apprentice contestant Josh Shaw at GoSMILE, a startup oral care company. Charged with building the company's Direct Response division and launching on television, web and the Home Shopping Network,

Chris's efforts helped pave the way for explosive success. GoSMILE became the one of the fastest-growing prestige brands in HSN's history, selling over $1.2 Million in the first 24 hours on air. Chris has been featured in various publications for his work in the Direct Response industry, including a cover story in trade flagship "DIRECT" Magazine highlighting his success at GoSMILE.

After his homerun at GoSMILE, Chris joined forces yet again with Shaw and fellow entrepreneurs to establish a new standard in the world of athletic retail with the launch of MISSION Athletecare, the first line of performance and recovery products designed and developed by the world's best professional athletes, including Dwyane Wade, Serena Williams, Sergio Garcia, Georges St-Pierre and more. In the company's first 5 years, retail sales have already exceeded $50 Million.

Chris is a Special Advisor to Texas A&M University's "Startup Aggieland" organization through the Mays Business School, which offers 24-7 access to student-startup offices and co-working spaces for student collaboration, as well as free business counseling, business programs and networking events for up and coming entrepreneurs. Chris is also the Chairman of the Health & Wellness Committee for the NFL Alumni Organization (NY/NJ), a charitable organization that serves as a passionate advocate for greater quality of life benefits for all former NFL players. He lives in New York City with his wife, Liliana, and son, John David.

**BUSINESS
BOOKS**

Business Books encapsulates the freshest thinkers and the most
successful practitioners in the areas of marketing, management,
economics, finance and accounting, sustainable and ethical
business, heart business, people management, leadership,
motivation, biographies, business recovery and development
and personal/executive development.